THEBES, *The Broken Obelisk c1857* 1896

Francis Frith's

EGYPT AND THE HOLY LAND

The Pioneering Photographic Expeditions to the Middle East

with an introduction and notes by RICHARD LUNN
and additional modern photographs

The Francis Frith Collection

First published in the United Kingdom in 2005 by
The Francis Frith Collection®

Hardback Edition Published in 2005 ISBN 1-85937-793-9

British Library Cataloguing in Publication Data

Francis Frith's Egypt and the Holy Land
Introduction and Notes by Richard Lunn

Modern photographs by Richard Lunn,
except where stated.
Image C711008 on page 151 reproduced by kind permission of the British Library.
Image ZZZ00151 on page 151 reproduced by kind permission of the British Museum.
Modern photographs of the Holy Land reproduced by kind permission of Todd Bolen/Bibleplaces.com

The Francis Frith Collection®
Frith's Barn, Teffont,
Salisbury, Wiltshire SP3 5QP
Tel: +44 (0) 1722 716 376
Email: info@francisfrith.co.uk
www.francisfrith.co.uk

Printed and bound in India

Front Cover: IBRIM, *Traveller's Boat c1857* 647E

AS WITH ANY HISTORICAL DATABASE THE FRITH ARCHIVE IS CONSTANTLY BEING CORRECTED AND IMPROVED AND THE PUBLISHERS WOULD WELCOME INFORMATION ON OMISSIONS OR INACCURACIES

The Transcription of ancient Egyptian, Arabic and Hebrew names

Ancient Egyptian, Arabic and Hebrew all share a common writing structure, in that in everyday writing many vowel sounds are not indicated. In addition, Arabic contains sounds that do not exist in English, and the sound structure of Ancient Egyptian has been reconstructed through cross referencing to Coptic, a late form of the language, and Greek transcriptions of names. This means there is a certain amount of confusion in how names of kings, gods and places should be spelt in English.

When Francis Frith was writing his text, there was no standardised form at all, and so he constructed his spelling based on the sound of words. Today, there is some degree of conformity, although different countries tend to use somewhat different spellings. For example, 'Rameses' tends to be spelt with two 'e's in British journals, whereas American journals tend to spell it 'Ramses' with just one 'e'.

Every attempt has been made to standardise the spellings in the recently written sections of this book, whilst Frith's transcriptions have been retained in his own captions and text.

Contents

Introduction

Francis Frith – His Own Words and Photographs

Appendices

Francis Frith, Pioneer Photographer and Explorer

Francis Frith 1822–1898

FRANCIS FRITH is one of the pioneers of photography; his early fame largely rested on these images of Egypt and the Holy Land. He was one of the first to develop the photographic postcard, which derived from the Victorian passion for the carte de visite (although he died in 1898, a year after a single-size format was introduced, and four years before the development of the divided back which we recognise today). His later fame rests very much on the record he began of Britain in the 19th century, although the 1886 catalogue of his company's images, which runs to 670 pages, includes photographs of most European countries as well as the USA, Canada, China and Japan.

When he was only in his thirties, Francis Frith began a series of trips to Egypt which lasted from 1857 until 1860. He penetrated beyond the sixth cataract, one of the first Europeans, and certainly the first photographer, to do so, although images only exist of monuments as far south as the second cataract. His reputation was based upon these early journeys. Indeed, in his time these explorations and the photographs that resulted from them were famous; Frith lectured extensively on the use of the new collodion process in hot climates, and his images were widely seen in an array of publications. He published an essay entitled 'The Art of Photography' in the 'Art Journal' of 1859, a summary of his beliefs about the status of the craft. He makes it plain that he believes that it is the truthfulness of the photograph that makes it so important.

When Francis Frith arrived at Alexandria in 1857 to trace the course of the Nile southwards, he was following in the footsteps of many illustrious earlier tourists and emulating the journeys of travellers dating back to 460 BC. It can justly be claimed that as well as providing us with the first beer, the first writing, a twelve-hour day, and the first stone-built buildings, the ancient Egyptians had an influence on the development of tourism.

From the earliest times Egypt seems to have instilled a sense of awe in the outsider. One of our first indications of this comes from a remarkable series of letters found at El-Amarna, the capital of the 'heretic king', Akhenaten. They were found by Egyptian diggers probably in 1887, and consisted of clay tablets inscribed for the most part in cuneiform Akkidian; they proved to be the diplomatic correspondence of the pharaohs over a period spanning three reigns, those of Amenhotep III, Akhenaten and Tutankhamun. The land of Egypt in some of these letters is clearly the land of fabled wealth and plenty that drew both Alexander the Great and Julius Caesar to it in much later times. In one (BM 29791), Tushratta, king of the kingdom of the Mittani, writes urging Pharaoh to send him gold: 'May my brother send me in very great quantities gold that has not been worked, and may my brother send me much more gold than he did to my father. In my brother's country it is as plentiful as dirt.' (Translation from 'The Amarna Letters', William L Moran). Egypt was the major power at this time in the region, and was seen very much as the fountain of prosperity. Clearly here we have an early example of the idea that the streets were paved with gold!

When Frith took his image of the step pyramid at Saqqara, he was not to know that below the sand lay evidence of tourism of a much earlier time. In the so-called House of the North are examples of New Kingdom 'tourist' graffiti, one of which states that the monument was 'as if heaven were within it' (S737002k). The ancients' idea of their past was not that dissimilar to the one of modern travellers. Later, for the Greeks, Egypt represented (in part at least) a source of ancient wisdom. Herodotus, Solon, and Pythagoras are all supposed to have used these sources. Herodotus, indeed, can lay claim to being the first tourist, and the long section on Egypt in his 'Histories' is some of the first travel writing. However, it is also clear from the writings of Herodotus that Egypt was also seen as being very different and rather unexplainably exotic; in many ways it was a kind of reverse Greece. Here it was the men who wove, while the women worked in fields. Men urinated sitting, while the women did so standing up. In this he was creating an image of an exotic other world, which to a greater or lesser extent has been with us ever since.

ABOVE: SAKKARAH (SAQQARA), *Tourist Graffiti at the Step Pyramid 2004*
S737002K

Francis Frith, Pioneer Photographer and Explorer

The Greeks and the Romans seem to have been in awe of the length of Egyptian history, their monuments, and their medical knowledge. For example, Imhotep, the builder of the step pyramid at Saqqara, became associated with the Greek god of healing, Asklepios, and was revered in Ptolemaic times. Cleopatra VII, in order to impress Julius Caesar, whose power she saw as protection for Egypt, took him on the ancient equivalent of the Nile cruise, travelling down the river to show him the sites of the ancient kingdom. Certainly, this same awe, inspired by the vast span of Egyptian history and the many wonders to be found in the country, was to be felt by Francis Frith two thousand years later.

Frith was an early photographer of Egypt and the Holy Land, but he records a time when the area was being examined by Western powers in an increasingly thorough, if at times destructive, way. Many monuments were being seen as quarries for antiquities for the museums of Europe, and adventurers such as Belzoni vied with each other to transport material home. Howard Vyse, an officer in the Royal Engineers, had used dynamite to blast his way into the pyramid of Menkaure at Giza in 1837.

SAKKARAH (SAQQARA), *The Step Pyramid 2004* S737004K

Traditionally Egypt had been the last stop in a grand tour of the Holy Land. It was thus seen very much from a Biblical perspective: it was the location of the Israelites' captivity, and a place of refuge for the fleeing Holy Family. Indeed, a brief survey of subscribers to the first part of the Frith collection of images of Egypt reveals that the third most numerous group of subscribers, after mere 'Mr', or figures associated with a university, were seventeen men of the cloth. Frith himself saw the visits he paid to Jerusalem and other sites associated with the Bible as tremendously important. Frith published his early collections in monthly instalments, each containing his text, and three images – one from Egypt, one from the Holy Land, and a third chosen from one of the two areas.

Until the 1830s, when a consensus was reached over the deciphering of hieroglyphs, a detailed and reasonably accurate historical analysis of ancient Egypt was not possible, but after this date there was a scramble by the colonial powers to obtain inscribed material for study in their academic institutions. As well as furthering the knowledge of the ancient language and civilisation, this resulted in many monuments being damaged in situ, and so the images Frith took can shed light on undamaged temples and locations.

First-hand experience of the country was beginning to be more widespread in the 19th century. The invasion by Napoleon and his

subsequent defeat by the British led to the opening up of the country. Napoleon's invasion was not simply military, but also a huge investigation into the past and the present of the country; the impact of the monumental 'Description de L'Égypt' (1809–1822), written by the scholars accompanying the expedition, was as immense as the book itself. Painters, artists, and architects now had at their disposal a huge source book of a complete and hitherto rather ill-documented civilisation. The impact on the Imperial style of the French court was massive, with sphinxes and other Egyptian motifs abounding in architecture and interior decoration.

In England the impact of the French expedition was also great, partly through the translations of Denon published in the early years of the

SAKKARAH (SAQQARA), *The Step Pyramid 2004* S737003K

century. There were many rival publications of his 'Travels in Upper and Lower Egypt during the Campaign of General Bonaparte'. The earliest I can find is dated 1802, published by James Ridgeway and translated by Francis Blagdon. In 1803 Longman & Rees Phillips published a translation by Arthur Aikin; other rival volumes appeared in 1807, 1809, and 1825. In the field of the decorative arts and architecture, the work of Owen Jones and his 'Grammar of Ornament', which was a compendium of architectural styles from the then known world including Egypt, became influential. The book was published in 1856, the year Frith left for Egypt, and was the first to give due prominence to styles dating from before the Greeks.

In Britain, Egypt came to be seen as strategically important, and in the early 1840s a new route to India was opened, known as the Overland Route. Thomas Waghorn linked Alexandria with Suez by way of Cairo with hotels such as Shepheard's in Cairo to provide for the traveller. This brought the wonders of the civilisation to a new educated administrative class. It should not be forgotten either that in the 1860s Thomas Cook founded the first package holiday firm on the basis of his cruises up the Nile, and these became increasingly popular amongst the mid to late Victorians. Egypt can be seen as the founding location of the modern holiday experience.

It is no coincidence that many Egyptian-style mausoleums in Kensal Green cemetery in north-west London (L1305710k, page 10), and the circle of Lebanon in Highgate, date from this time. Some of the more wealthy visitors were able to take a cruise in relative comfort down the Nile to wonder at the ruins of the past, and the images they brought back,

LONDON, *An Uninscribed Tomb, Kensal Green 2004* L1305710K

or bought in England, provided a model for cemetery architecture at a time when 'garden cemeteries' were seen as providing a solution to the problem of burial in towns.

That Egypt began to open up at this time is not solely due to the colonising spirit of the age. The rulers and the ordinary people of the country were not without some power. Mohammed Ali, the Viceroy from 1806 until 1849, had been born in Albania, and was keen to see his country modernised, which even then meant in his mind westernised. He encouraged investment and expertise from Britain and France; Belzoni went to Egypt initially to sell an irrigation pump. Emily M Weeks, in her essay 'About-Face: Sir David Wilkie's Portrait of Mehemet Ali', offers an interesting analysis of the painting, which emphasised the power that the ruler actually had. We should not fall into the trap of imagining that the Egyptians were passive recipients of the growing colonisation from the west.

In Frith's time, David Roberts had done much to popularise paintings of Egypt following his journeys, which began in 1838. Indeed, Frith explicitly acknowledges Roberts's influence in his writings about the Rameseum, mentioning his 'splendid work'. Edward Lear visited the country in 1854; Gustave Flaubert from 1849 to 1851; and Florence Nightingale from 1849 to 1850. Egypt under the more pro-European rulers Mohammed Ali and Said Pasha was certainly opening up to the west.

Frith seems to have been influenced in several ways by the work of other artists, and the intellectual movements of his day. He was living in a time of great change and debate in matters scientific, aesthetic and theological. Frith's recorded interests included the philosophers John

Locke, Adam Smith, and Joseph Butler. These thinkers stressed the empirical nature of knowledge, the primacy of the real world, and the value of observation. They did not, however, let this lead to religious doubt; although Frith did have a crisis of faith at nineteen, he also resolved this by a belief in the testable and observable evidence for God. That the pictures of the Holy Land and Jerusalem in particular can be read as affirmations of his faith is not to be doubted.

However, in 1830 Charles Lyell produced his influential work 'Principles of Geology', which in its insistence on the vast age of the rocks contradicted the Biblical story of creation. It also led to an aesthetic interest in rock formation articulated by Ruskin, and evident in the work of some painters such as Alfred William Hunt, John Brett, and John William Inchbold. These images may well have had an influence on some of Frith's images, as Inchbold and Brett were both exhibited in Liverpool in the early 1850s, where Frith was living at the time. Although Frith's interest in recording images of the Sinai region stemmed from the fact that this was in the Biblical Holy Land, photographs such as 'Sinai, The Wadee el-Mukattab' (525, page 176) and 'Sinai, Sinaitic Inscriptions in Wadee el-Mukattab' (526, page 177) seem to owe their formal composition to the ideas and work of Ruskin and these painters of landscape.

In 1859, a year after Frith's first publication of images of Egypt and Palestine, Darwin published 'The Origin of Species by Natural Selection', which ignited a growing debate about the literal truth of the Bible. Frith's photographs were in part taken to record the scientific truth of the Holy Land, and were seen by him to be superior to painting. In his own mind at least, they were evidence for the veracity of the Bible stories, and therefore a way of dealing with the new uncertainties of the mid 19th century; the growing market for such images suggests that he was not alone in this view.

Frith was not the first photographer to use the new collodion process in the Middle East. James Graham, one-time organiser of the office in Jerusalem of the London Society for Promoting Christianity amongst the Jews, began taking images of Jerusalem and the Holy Land using this process only two years after it had been invented in 1851. His aims were very much the same as Frith's, and he accompanied William Holman Hunt in his painting tour of Egypt and the Holy Land. In March 1857 he was in Egypt photographing the pyramids, which places him as an exact contemporary of Frith, who was also in Egypt in 1857. In 1859 Graham exhibited his images in Paris accompanied by titles drawn from scripture, where they were widely praised.

Frith, in common with most travellers of his day, travelled by sea to Alexandria; after a turbulent journey from England, he arrived in late 1856. Frith and his technical collaborator, Francis Wenham, were then conveyed to Cairo, where a boat was bargained for. Frith's account of his arrival in Alexandria in 'A True Story' captures the sense of wonder, bewilderment and exhilaration that most travellers seem to have felt: 'Alexandria was the greatest "sensation" that I had ever experienced. Even at this distance of time, the mere recollection of it is thrilling. There was positively nothing that I had seen before, except perhaps a general likeness in the people to human form. I had seen what we in England call sunshine, but it was nothing like the vital, almost tangible stuff that made itself part and parcel of the dust and stones and atmosphere of Alexandria ... Donkeys and donkey boys had formerly been, in my eyes, very vulgar and sleepy institutions: not so were they by any means. [I had] a scuffle with an army of them, and a triumphant ride, at full gallop, through the narrow crowded streets to the European Square, upon a chosen specimen named John Bright, impelled by a running commentary of the wildest type of Jingoism, whose extravagant and frantic yells and blows I was utterly unable, paralysed as I was with outrageous merriment and laughter, in the least degree to control.'

This echoes a piece written in 1849 by the businessman Samuel Bevan, who helped Thomas Waghorne establish the Overland Route to India through Egypt: 'I shall never forget the scene that awaited us on landing at the hard. Camels, donkeys, merchandise of every description, shrieking women, boys, and greasy Arabs all jumbled together in indescribable confusion ... off we went at a gallop with a boy at each tail, through some narrow streets, between high walls.'

In contrast, Frith's description of the island of Philae is poetic and gentle in the extreme: 'Philae is the most beautiful thing in Egypt; and the temple, absurdly called Pharaoh's Bed, is the most beautiful thing upon the island. I flatter myself, too, somewhat upon the quality of my Photograph, – light transparent shadows, sweet half-tones, oh discriminating public! It is true that the temple outdoes the Tower of Babel, not only "reaching unto the heavens" but robbing the picture of well-nigh all its sky.'

Something seems to have happened on the journey: a poetic spirit is released. This tension in his writing between an urge to admire and a feeling of bewilderment exists on many levels, and echoes travellers' reactions to Egypt from Herodotus onwards.

As an Egyptologist, one of the most vivid impressions of my life is undoubtedly the morning of my own first visit to Egypt. I had booked a late cruise in high summer, partly because it was cheap, and partly because of my interest in ancient Egypt. We arrived at Aswan airport, then a converted military shed, at about two in the morning. There was a gasp from the passengers as the pilot announced that the outside temperature was 32°C. It was dark and very hot outside, and so we could not get any impression of the country that night.

The next morning the cruise ship was under way along the Nile. I woke around seven thirty and pulled the curtains of the cabin to one side. What I saw will stay with me forever. The river was like a dark mirror, beyond which rose a line of olive green vegetation wearing a row of palm trees above it. Beyond that the rich yellow desert cliffs gently diffused into the pink of early morning. I was hit by a hot wind, but stood in amazement at what I saw. People were already up and by the river washing pots, tending cattle, bathing, and fishing. The torn white rags of egrets flapped lazily against the green of the vegetation. The overwhelming impression was one of tranquillity, and a sense of timelessness. My only regret is that I can never see this for the first time again. On subsequent trips, often showing friends around the historic sites, their reaction is similar to mine; Egypt casts a spell. This spell seems to have strengthened its hold on Frith as he made his way up the Nile from Cairo to Aswan.

However, before Frith was able to reach the south of the country, various hurdles had to be overcome in Cairo. He rented a dahibieh, or sailing ship, for £30 a month with an eleven-man crew included. He and Wenham then set sail for the south and the second cataract at Wadi Halfa.

THE ISLAND OF PHILAE, *A Ruined Mosque 1857* 1817E

Francis Frith, Pioneer Photographer and Explorer

The going was slower than expected owing to the lack of wind, but eventually their goal was achieved, and they began their photography. (The images of Egypt in this volume are arranged from the south to the north of Egypt, roughly following Frith's journey).

Not only do Frith's images shed light on the ancient past of Egypt, but also on the times in which the images were created. Egypt was viewed in many complex and often contradictory ways in 19th-century Europe. On the one hand there was admiration for its history and artistic achievement, reflected by the artists of the period; on the other there was a recognition that this achievement was pagan, and that this country was the one from which the Israelites escaped. Modern Egypt was also a land which was considered to be inferior in many ways to ancient Egypt; 19th-century westerners thought that this was partly because of the Egyptians' oriental lethargy, and partly because of their religion.

At this time, fine art with Egyptian or Biblical themes was very popular, and there was an increase in the general public's interest in the archaeology and history of the region. David Roberts's engravings had been published in instalments during 1848 and 1849, and they were then bound in two large volumes. This clearly influenced the publication of Frith's images, which adopted the same format. In his comments on a photograph of the Temple of Rameses II, Frith compares his image to that of Roberts: 'David Roberts in his splendid work has bestowed upon it a very respectable and recognisable profile; but my picture shows that the face is so mutilated as scarcely to leave a feature traceable.' The status of the new scientific process of photography is seen as both arising from the work of engravers such as Roberts, and also as being more truthful.

Another artist of the same period was Jacob Jacobs, a Belgian painter who visited Egypt in the 1830s and came to England in 1855 to exhibit his paintings of Karnak and other Egyptian views. An almost exact contemporary of Frith was the French painter Gérôme, who painted views of the colossi of Memnon in 1857, the same year that Frith was in Egypt. It is interesting to compare Gerome's painting with Frith's photograph of the same subject (1857, page 122): the foreground of both painting and photograph is occupied by a very similar camel encampment. Roberts too had produced a view of the colossi, which seems to provide Frith with his basic viewpoint. Edward Lear, famous for painting, illustration and poetry, visited Egypt in 1846. His pictures of Philae are dated 1854, and it is

ABOVE: GIZA, *The Pyramids, from an engraving* ZZZ01425

possible that Frith may have seen these images before his trips to the Middle East.

What seems certain is that Frith saw himself in the tradition of these artists, although for its truthfulness Frith clearly thought photography superior. The introduction to Frith's one hundred stereoscopic views, written by Samuel Sharpe, states: 'The Valley of the Nile has been visited by a variety of travellers, who have brought home drawings of the buildings made under various difficulties. Denon, following the French army, published a volume of views; but too often sketched hastily, perhaps while his comrades were engaged in battle. The scientific expedition sent out by Napoleon was accompanied by several artists; but their costly volumes too clearly show that the drawings received many of their last touches in Paris. Some of our English artists have also published beautiful volumes of the picturesque ruins in this land, most interesting for the draftsman; but we cannot but sometimes fancy that they have sacrificed somewhat of scientific accuracy to artistic effect. But when we look at photographic views we are troubled by no such misgivings. Here we have all the truthfulness of nature, all the reality of the objects themselves, and at the same time, artistic effects which leave nothing to wish for.'

Here again we see that scientific claims are being made for the new process. It was thought to show reality, rather than an artist's impression. Ruskin had already urged artists to paint with a new attention to detail, and this advice had been followed by the new pre-Raphaelite movement. Holman Hunt, a leading pre-Raphaelite, himself travelled to Egypt and the Holy Land to paint.

Although the text accompanying Frith's photographs is well researched, relying somewhat heavily on classical sources and Sir John Gardiner Wilkinson's 'Manners and Customs of the Ancient Egyptians' (published by Murray in 1836), it is clear that Frith's primary concern was aesthetic; on visiting Dashur he wrote: 'In the earliest times when the pyramids were perfect, their appearance must have been far less picturesque, from the want of variety of form in their structure.'

In the Victorian period, ancient Egypt was increasingly seen as a precursor to Greek civilisation, not least because the Greeks themselves had acknowledged the debt. However, as an African civilisation it caused Europeans some problems at this time. To justify the colonisation of the 'dark continent', a myth of an undeveloped and backward continent had to be created, and the African nature of aspects of Egyptian civilisation were difficult to explain. Continuity with modern Egypt was denied, and so ancient Egypt came to be seen in a kind of isolation, a unique and separate case from the rest of the continent and from the modern world.

Thus many images, such as some by David Roberts or W H Bartlett, seem partly to ignore the Egypt of their day, or if they do record it, they show a mysterious and decadent 'oriental' world. Frith's images, on the other hand, include many of mid 19th-century Cairo, and they also portray local inhabitants in views of the monuments. His later well-documented concern for everyday social life in England seems to be prefigured by these images of Egypt.

In the Holy Land, Frith seems to have intended to provide a scientific record of the places mentioned in the Bible. He was, of course, aware of the commercial opportunities a publication of this nature would provide, but his main aim was certainly to add material to the growing debates surrounding the truth of the biblical accounts. There seems to be something of a contrast between the attitudes of Frith and those of some of his near contemporary travellers to the country and people of Egypt. In general, Frith seems to have been entranced by both the country and the people. He talks of a 'vivid orientalism' which 'never deserted or failed' him. His account of the view of the tombs in the Southern Cemetery in Cairo is factual and accurate, sensitive to the present population and their unconscious echoes of the ancients: 'We may, in imagination, see the long files of mourners winding over the plain (not unlike the ancient Egyptian trains that carried the dead across this very tract).'

In a letter from Holman Hunt, written during his nearly contemporary visit to Cairo in 1854, we gain a very different impression: 'It is the horrible state of dilapidation in which one finds everything that disgusts so much.' Later we read of Hunt's attitude to the locals: 'You would be astonished by their want of courage; when we in walking come upon a party of natives who do not at once get out of our way, at our expostulation with them, we raise our sticks and lay about on ten or twenty together.' In an account of Amelia Edwards's trip up the Nile written by Jennie Lane, we hear an account of how a Mr Eyre shot a boy of seven, who luckily was 'not badly hurt. A few shots went into his body and one or two into his head and face.' It is hardly surprising that the boy's father and the village were angered by this, and attacked the English party. A few days later it was the Egyptians who were punished with a sound beating, under orders from the governor of Aswan. 'I don't suppose they will want to attack another English gentleman', writes Jennie.

In contrast, for the most part Frith simply seems captivated by the mystery of the land: 'Each morning I awoke to a fresh and joyous consciousness that I was breathing the brighter and freer atmosphere, as it were, of another planet.' He seems to have been sucked into the Egyptian way of life, and despite being a devout Quaker, he is remarkably open to the lure of the pagan: 'I am more tempted to worship a crocodile thirty feet long and five hundred or a thousand years old, than to bow down to the God of Calvin; the former seems to me to be the finer and nobler conception of the two.' Again, in talking of the people, he says: 'I have spent months, fearing no evil, amongst men whom we call real savages ... whose souls appear to be, if anything, rather more religiously enlightened than is the soul of an average, modern scientific professor.' This remarkable

ABOVE: CAIRO, *Tombs in the Southern Cemetery c1857* 1966

contrast between Frith's attitudes and those of his contemporaries was perhaps brought about through Frith's faith, and perhaps by the habit of deep and sensitive observation that a great photographer has to apply.

Although he does seem to have more sympathy with the local country and its people than many Europeans, this somewhat uncharacteristic outburst is to be found in the text accompanying the image of Dendera: '... one can explore and admire without being subjected to the odious concomitants of Arab filth and Arab impertinence.' Here there is a hint of some problems with the population that seem reasonably rare in his writing, but Frith's words indicate the bemusement felt by many travellers when they contrasted the glories of the past and the apparent squalor of the 19th century. In the final analysis, Frith was also a man of his time – he writes: 'It is an exciting thought that perhaps to England will eventually fall the task of governing this wonderful land, and reviewing and Christianising its mummied and paralysed life.'

GEEZEH (GIZA), *Khufu Pyramid 2004* G318004

The Technical Aspects of the Images and their Publication

AS WELL as being an innovator in terms of the content of the images he produced, Francis Frith was also a technical innovator. He adopted the then new collodion process, which had only been introduced in 1851, six years before his journey to Egypt. It was invented by Frederick Scott Archer, and the process used guncotton dissolved in ether and alcohol. It provided a relatively stable bond in the form of a thin film between the light-sensitive chemicals and the glass plate. This meant that an image could be made which was as sharp as the daguerreotype, but which could be reproduced in the same way as a calotype. A further advantage was that it was more sensitive to light, allowing shorter exposure times.

Frith's companion, Francis Wenham, was an inventor and an early theorist of flight. He almost certainly worked with Frith on the lenses needed to produce the sharp images. This new technology probably accounts for the appearance of local Egyptians in many of Frith's photographs: the relatively short exposure time allowed for the presence of human figures, which were usually excluded – their movements would make an unsightly blur. When we see such assured photographs, it is easy to forget how early they occur in the history of the art. One indication that Frith was breaking new ground is that William Fox Talbot, the earliest English practitioner of photography, used a stereo image of Edfu taken by Frith to illustrate one of his own lectures on photography. Frith was truly a pioneer. What makes the achievement of Francis Frith in Egypt remarkable is his reliance on water to produce a wet plate; in the extreme heat of the country, this is no small achievement. Not only that, but the chemicals he used were highly explosive. Thus when we contemplate the photographer working in something like a mobile laboratory, dealing with very unstable chemicals in the heat of the Egyptian desert, we can feel nothing less than admiration.

We forget that the size of the camera and the plates used by Frith would have made the journey and the actual taking of the images extremely difficult. T Frederick Hardwich saw Frith taking images in England: 'His plates were so large that when I first saw him developing a negative it looked like a man balancing the top of a small table on his fingers and pouring a jug of water over it.' Once in Egypt, Frith had to manage three cameras: a stereo camera, a whole-plate camera, and a mammoth plate camera that was so large that it needed its own covered vehicle. Let us not forget, too, that for Frith there was no small and light film stock, with enough 35mm film for a two-week trip fitting into a large pocket. His negatives were large and bulky plates of glass, which had to be transported with the rest of the equipment along with the chemicals to develop the images on site. Heat and dust provided problems with the wet plates, and caused the appearance of pinholes on the developed images. Not only that, but the atmosphere inside the tent he worked in must have been almost unbearable. All light and therefore air had to be excluded, and in temperatures well over one hundred degrees Fahrenheit, Frith himself describes the situation as 'the suffocating heat of the small tent'. The technical expertise of Wenham, who certainly helped a great deal on this first trip, is unrecorded by Frith, although from Wenham's own writings it is clear that he assisted Frith with the developing process.

Frith put his first collection on the market between 1858 and 1860. Seventy-six prints were published in twenty-five parts. They were collected under the title 'Egypt and Palestine. Photographed and described by Francis Frith'. In this early volume Frith wrote the descriptions himself,

Part 21. PRICE TEN SHILLINGS.

PHOTOGRAPHED AND DESCRIBED

BY

F. FRITH, JUN.

LONDON:
JAMES S. VIRTUE, CITY ROAD AND IVY LANE;
AND 26, JOHN STREET, NEW YORK.

and the images were largely of Upper Egypt in the area of Luxor, Aswan and Nubia, and of Nazareth, Baalbec and Jerusalem. The publisher was James Virtue, a long-established publisher of maps and books of engravings. In 1847 they had published Henry Stebbing's 'A Christian in Palestine', a book which also contained engravings of the region by W H Bartlett. Bartlett was a prolific illustrator who, somewhat earlier than Frith, seems to have had a similar career of publishing views from around the world. In the mid 1850s Bartlett produced a book of views of Egypt, 'The Nile Boat, or Glimpses of the Land of Egypt', some of which foreshadow those by Frith. Whether Frith knew that his experiment would be a success or not is open to debate. There is no doubt that it was a risky venture, and also that there were profound personal reasons for the trip to lands so intimately linked with Bible stories. However, as Virtue had already made a success of W H Bartlett's work, and the format of the relatively cheap regular editions had been introduced with some of David Roberts's work, it might seem that precedents for the commercial success of this kind of publication already existed.

In 1860 a new set of photographs was published: the Egyptian images were nearly all of Cairo and the pyramids, with many images of sites in Sinai. For this production Sophia Poole and her younger son Reginald were employed to write the descriptions. Sophia had travelled to Egypt in 1842, and had stayed there for seven years. She published a book called

LEFT: PORTFOLIO COVER, *from Frith's Portfolio of his Photographs of Egypt and Palestine*

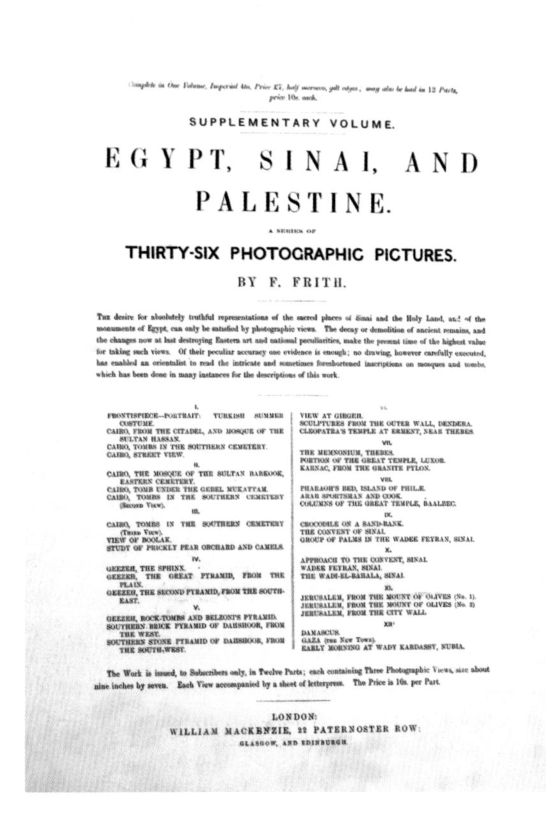
Complete in One Volume, Imperial 4to, Price £7, half morocco, gilt edges; may also be had in 12 Parts, price 10s. each.

SUPPLEMENTARY VOLUME.

EGYPT, SINAI, AND PALESTINE.

A SERIES OF

THIRTY-SIX PHOTOGRAPHIC PICTURES.

BY F. FRITH.

The desire for absolutely truthful representations of the sacred places of Sinai and the Holy Land, and of the monuments of Egypt, can only be satisfied by photographic views. The decay or demolition of ancient remains, and the changes now at last destroying Eastern art and national peculiarities, make the present time of the highest value for taking such views. Of their peculiar accuracy one evidence is enough; no drawing, however carefully executed, has enabled an orientalist to read the intricate and sometimes foreshortened inscriptions on mosques and tombs, which has been done in many instances for the descriptions of this work.

I.

FRONTISPIECE—PORTRAIT: TURKISH SUMMER COSTUME.
CAIRO, FROM THE CITADEL, AND MOSQUE OF THE SULTAN HASSAN.
CAIRO, TOMBS IN THE SOUTHERN CEMETERY.
CAIRO, STREET VIEW.

II.

CAIRO, THE MOSQUE OF THE SULTAN BARKOOK, EASTERN CEMETERY.
CAIRO, TOMB UNDER THE GEBEL MUKATTAM.
CAIRO, TOMBS IN THE SOUTHERN CEMETERY (SECOND VIEW).

III.

CAIRO, TOMBS IN THE SOUTHERN CEMETERY (THIRD VIEW).
VIEW OF BOOLAK.
STUDY OF PRICKLY PEAR ORCHARD AND CAMELS.

IV.

GEEZEH, THE SPHINX.
GEEZEH, THE GREAT PYRAMID, FROM THE PLAIN.
GEEZEH, THE SECOND PYRAMID, FROM THE SOUTH-EAST.

V.

GEEZEH, ROCK-TOMBS AND BELZONI'S PYRAMID.
SOUTHERN BRICK PYRAMID OF DAHSHOOR, FROM THE WEST.
SOUTHERN STONE PYRAMID OF DAHSHOOR, FROM THE SOUTH-WEST.

VI.

VIEW AT GIRGEH.
SCULPTURES FROM THE OUTER WALL, DENDERA.
CLEOPATRA'S TEMPLE AT ERMENT, NEAR THEBES.

VII.

THE MEMNONIUM, THEBES.
PORTION OF THE GREAT TEMPLE, LUXOR.
KARNAC, FROM THE GRANITE PYLON.

VIII.

PHARAOH'S BED, ISLAND OF PHILÆ.
ARAB SPORTSMAN AND COOK.
COLUMNS OF THE GREAT TEMPLE, BAALBEC.

IX.

CROCODILE ON A SAND-BANK.
THE CONVENT OF SINAI.
GROUP OF PALMS IN THE WADEE FEYRAN, SINAI.

X.

APPROACH TO THE CONVENT, SINAI.
WADEE FEYRAN, SINAI.
THE WADI-EL-BAHALA, SINAI.

XI.

JERUSALEM, FROM THE MOUNT OF OLIVES (No. 1).
JERUSALEM, FROM THE MOUNT OF OLIVES (No. 2).
JERUSALEM, FROM THE CITY WALL.

XII.

DAMASCUS.
GAZA (THE NEW TOWN).
EARLY MORNING AT WADY KARDASSY, NUBIA.

The Work is issued, to Subscribers only, in Twelve Parts; each containing Three Photographic Views, size about nine inches by seven. Each View accompanied by a sheet of letterpress. The Price is 10s. per Part.

LONDON:
WILLIAM MACKENZIE, 22 PATERNOSTER ROW:
GLASGOW, AND EDINBURGH.

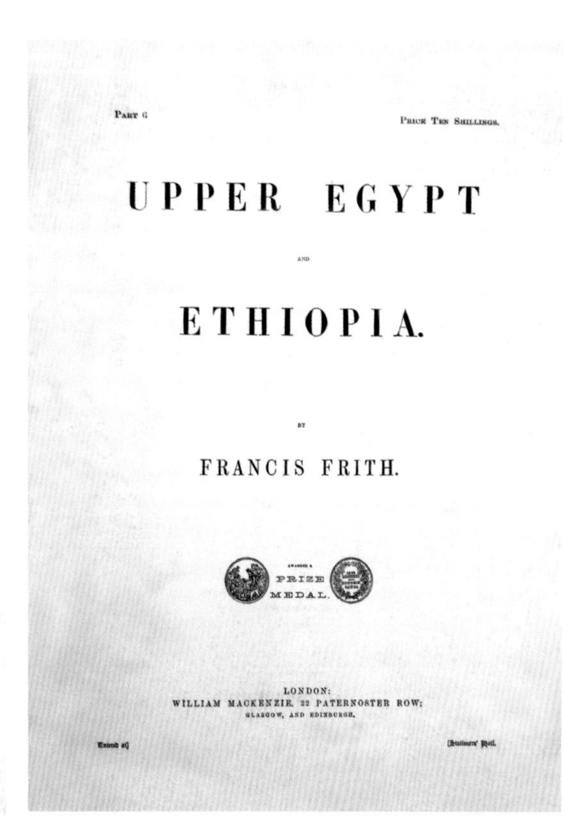
PART 6 PRICE TEN SHILLINGS.

UPPER EGYPT AND ETHIOPIA.

BY

FRANCIS FRITH.

AWARDED A PRIZE MEDAL.

LONDON:
WILLIAM MACKENZIE, 22 PATERNOSTER ROW;
GLASGOW, AND EDINBURGH.

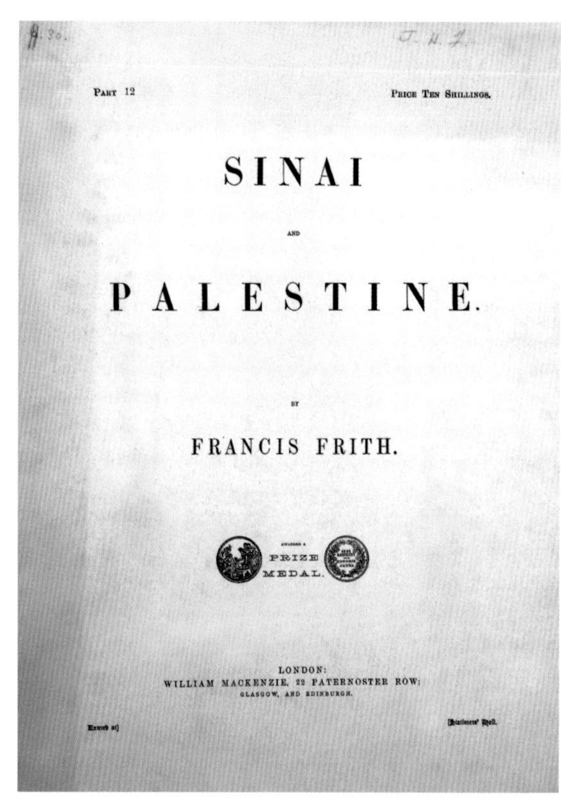
PART 12 PRICE TEN SHILLINGS.

SINAI AND PALESTINE.

BY

FRANCIS FRITH.

AWARDED A PRIZE MEDAL.

LONDON:
WILLIAM MACKENZIE, 22 PATERNOSTER ROW;
GLASGOW, AND EDINBURGH.

'An Englishwoman in Egypt', while Reginald became keeper of coins and medals at the British Museum.

ABOVE LEFT: PORTFOLIO BACK COVER, *from Frith's Portfolio of his Photographs of Egypt, Sinai and Palestine*

ABOVE CENTRE: PORTFOLIO COVER, *from Frith's Portfolio of his Photographs of Upper Egypt and Ethiopia*

ABOVE RIGHT: PORTFOLIO COVER, *from Frith's Portfolio of his Photographs of Sinai and Palestine*

In 1862 Frith published a volume of stereo images of Egypt with the snappy title of 'Egypt, Nubia and Ethiopia: illustrated by one hundred Stereoscopic Photographs taken by Francis Frith for Messrs Negretti and Zambra, with Descriptions and Numerous Wood Engravings by Joseph Bonomi and Notes by Samuel Sharpe'. Bonomi had spent from 1824 to 1834 in Egypt, and with Owen Jones had created the Egyptian Court at the Crystal Palace when it moved from Hyde Park to Sydenham. Samuel Sharpe is described as an orientalist, and a prolific one at that. He is best known for his 'History of Egypt from the Earliest Times till the Conquest by the Arabs AD 640'. This was first published in 1846, and underwent numerous revisions; it was last printed in 1905. He wrote early guides to the Egyptian antiquities in the British Museum and to the hieroglyphs of ancient Egypt.

From Frith's ability to call on the services of such well known Egyptologists of the time, we see that his work had gained a certain measure of academic as well as popular acclaim. Artistic acclaim arrived in 1861, when the stereoscopic prints won a medal at that year's Great Exhibition. There is no doubt that Frith was part of a movement that in the mid 19th century began to make the designs and history of Egypt and the Holy Land accessible, and in some quarters popular. In 1741 the Egyptian Society had been founded in London; its members included Lord Sandwich and Thomas Pococke. James Bruce was travelling in the country in 1772 and 1773, and in 1854 the Egyptian Court at the Crystal Palace was completed, designed by Owen Jones and Joseph Bonomi, who was to collaborate with Frith on his book of stereoscopic views.

The Egyptian Court was extremely well received; a review in the Gentleman's Magazine from June 1854 read: 'The Assyrian, Egyptian, Greek, Pompeian, and Alhambra courts are perfect reproductions of the finest specimens of work in their respective styles ... one of the finest effects is that of the pair of colossal Egyptian figures, with the avenue of sphinxes in the transepts at the northern end.' However, this fascination with the oriental had met with something of a backlash in the recent past. The Architectural Magazine of 1837 contained an article by J A Picton, which stated: 'It is very doubtful whether the Egyptian style is most appropriate

to a Christian burial place. It certainly has no connexion with our religion.' In his Royal Academy Lecture in 1852, C R Cockrell bemoaned the fact that Egyptian architecture was 'crude and primitive' and was linked with 'vile superstition'. He went on to mock the idea of 'a pylon in the streets of York, or London, or a Hypostyle in Covent Garden or Buckingham Palace.' Of course, two years after this talk there were queues forming to see the Egyptian Court at the Great Exhibition, where, as we have seen, the Egyptian Court had favourable reviews.

The influence of the Near East on the culture and art of the west has

ABOVE: LONDON, *The Crystal Palace c1886* C2071034

LONDON, *The Crystal Palace, The Water Tower c1861* 981

LONDON, *The Crystal Palace c1886* C2071013

always been ambiguous. Often buildings with entertainment or commercial uses have adopted Egyptian influences. The Carlton Cinema in Essex Road, Islington is the sole remaining example of a number of Egyptianised cinemas in England (L1305709k, page 25), whilst in Mornington Crescent there is the Carreras factory, which was opened on 3 November 1928. In 1988 there was considerable controversy over the building of a Homebase in Egyptian style in Kensington (K9701k, page 25). It was designed by Ian Pollard with hand-carved representations of Egyptian gods; but Sir John Sainsbury, chairman of Sainsbury's, then owners of Homebase, personally visited the site and ordered the destruction of the columns at the front before the building had been finished.

The most recent building I have seen in London using this style is the Four Seasons Hotel in Docklands. Designed by United Designers and with an interior by Philippe Starck, it was built by SISK, and stands elegantly on the bank of the Thames (L1305711k, right). Cockrell's worst fears are being realised!

There is no doubt that Francis Frith played his part in making the designs and lands of Egypt and Palestine accessible to wider public. By issuing the photographs in parts, the publisher allowed the spreading of the cost, and thus a wider audience could afford what was an expensive production. In this Frith was both reacting to an already established tradition, and also helping to extend and deepen it.

ABOVE LEFT: LONDON, *A Papyrus Bundle Column, Liverpool Street Station 2004* L1305707K

ABOVE RIGHT: LONDON, *Carreras Factory, Mornington Crescent 2004* L1305712K

BELOW: LONDON, *The Four Seasons Hotel, Docklands 2004* L1305711K

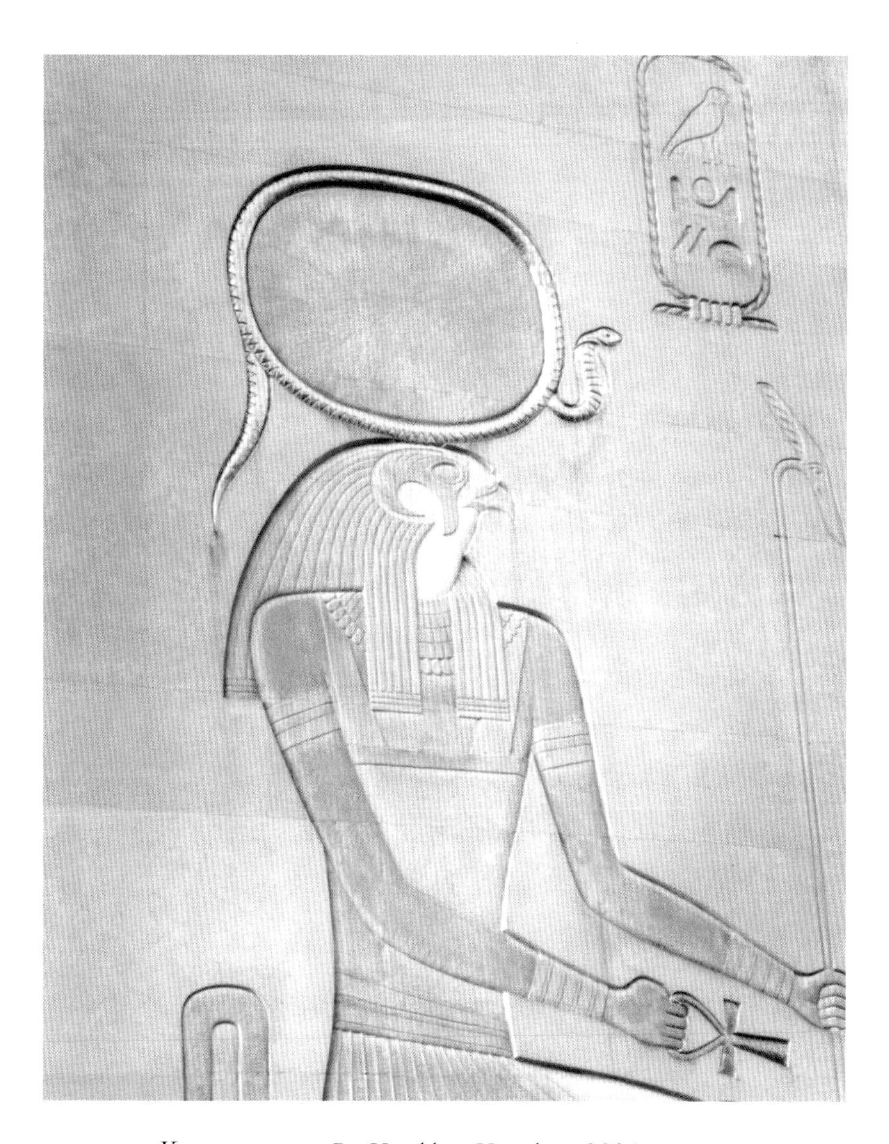

ABOVE LEFT: KENSINGTON, *Re-Horakhty, Homebase 2004* K9701K

RIGHT: LONDON, *A Papyrus Column on the Carlton Cinema, Islington 2004* L1305709K

Following in Frith's Footsteps through Modern Egypt

TO FOLLOW the journey of Francis Frith today through Egypt is not difficult, although the temples of the far south, such as the ones at Soleb, where he took some excellent images, are now in the Sudan, and not easily accessible. This immediately hints at one of the outstanding facts of Frith's journey: the immense distance he covered. From the south to the mosques of Cairo is by modern jet a journey of nearly two hours, and in that time the temperature changes remarkably. In spring Cairo is cool in the evening, with the daytime temperature about the same as a good English summer day; in the south the day begins at seven or eight o'clock, and the temperature climbs rapidly. By midday it is baking hot. For Frith to work here with volatile chemicals and no modern lightweight clothing is almost beyond belief. That he transported not only his huge cameras (the large plates used in one measured 20 inches by 16 inches) but also tents to live in and to use as a darkroom, is astounding. He talks of the bottles of the volatile chemicals popping like ginger beer, and bubbling on the plate.

Today all is much easier in many ways. A cruise boat will meet you at either Aswan or at Abu Simbel, and for three or four days you can cruise the isolated splendour of Lake Nasser. This modern lake has provided Egypt with a regular supply of water and immense amounts of cheap electricity; however, it has considerably altered the landscape and the microclimate of the area. None of the temples that Frith photographed here in the far south are in their original location; rather, they stand in open-air museums along the cruise route. The job of re-locating the temples has been done well by multi-national teams, and all the sites retain their dignity and grandeur. Landing on a beach by small boats far from any sign of habitation or vegetation to visit the temples is an awe-inspiring experience, but one which would have been unfamiliar to Frith. In his day the temples would not have seemed so remote, as the banks of the Nile between the first and second cataracts would have been populated by the Nubians. They have now been moved to new villages around Aswan, leaving the banks of the lake bare of people or cultivation. Crocodiles are still there, and it is possible to make friends with some of the smaller ones (N209010k, above).

The photographs of Qasr Ibrihim show best how much the Aswan High Dam has made the waters rise (I72001k, page 65, I72002k, page 28). The high bluff pictured by Frith is now a rather sad island, up to which the boat noses delicately. At times the lake is so wide that the banks are not visible, and for a few minutes the cruise boat sails out of sight of land.

ABOVE: NUBIA, *A Crocodile 2004* N209010K

NUBIA, *The Temple of Maharraka c1857* 1803

Following in Frith's Footsteps through Modern Egypt

The highlight of the journey is undoubtedly Abu Simbel, the huge rock-cut temple of the deified Rameses II. Here the Egyptians are as rightly proud of the moving of the temple in the 1960s as of its original construction. It now rests on an artificial hill built around a concrete dome, but it is still breathtaking. It soars above the viewer to the faces of the huge colossi, which seem to smile down in imperturbable power. In ancient times it marked one of the southern boundaries of the country, its message clear: 'This is the land of a king of great power'. Today it also marks a border, the border between Egypt and the Sudan. At Aswan the nature of this modern border became more obvious; at the station, groups of squatting Sudanese waited patiently and silently in the dust for the train or the coaches to take them south and home. It was here that a huge flock of pelicans circled the boat, their great white and yellow wings brilliant against the deep blue of the sky. Eagles and black kites, too, were common over the desert and the water.

The route beyond Aswan up the Nile today towards Luxor is accomplished most often by air-conditioned cruise boat, after a stop at the new site of the Philae temple. The journey across the water at dusk to the sound and light show is a highlight of any trip to Egypt. The temple is certainly one of the most perfect in Egypt, and the new location is remarkably faithful to the original. The road journey to Luxor takes three hours in an escorted convoy, while the flight takes less than half an hour. The airport, built in a style heavily influenced by ancient Egypt, is modern and very clean. There is even a direct flight here once a week from England; how much the world has shrunk since the time of Frith! I suspect that even Wenham would be amazed by our modern flying machines.

Luxor was bustling on our arrival. It was the spring festival of 'Sniffing the Breeze', a custom whose origins date to Pharaonic times, celebrated by a bank holiday in modern Egypt. It seemed that every inhabitant of Luxor had decided to emerge into the spring sun and set up a picnic site on the normally rather sedate Corniche. Large family groups with black-robed mothers and lively smiling children made progress very difficult. Young men posed and eyed the tourists and the girls as they do in any country, while a huge bustling market behind Luxor temple sold shiny souvenirs. This scene must have looked much the same when the ancient Egyptians came out to celebrate the end of the winter.

Today, the sites that Frith visited have been excavated and partially

RIGHT: IBRIM, *Qasr Ibrim 2004* I72002K

ABOVE: THEBES, *Luxor Temple, Image of Horemheb 2004* T323014K

reconstructed. This work is still in progress, and it made the photographing of an exact modern version of the original difficult. Frith could undoubtedly climb on the monuments at will, but the watchful eyes of the custodians and the Tourist and Antiquities Police today made this difficult. Nevertheless, it was exciting to work out the exact spot from which the 19th-century image was taken, and to imagine the presence of the tripod and heavy camera.

However, I feel that something of the romance of the half buried and decayed temples has been lost, and often now the central axis of Karnak is as crowded as a shopping precinct on a Saturday near Christmas. Despite this, it is possible to escape, as the tour groups stick to a fairly rigid itinerary. To take the modern images of the sculptural gateway (T323013K, page 30), we ventured far from the tourist route, and were rewarded by having the Temple of Khonsu to ourselves. We were thankful that this magnificent building was deserted. We quickly made friends with the two custodians, who ushered us up the stairs in the pylon gate on to the roof to take some pictures of the whole Karnak complex. Absolute secrecy was required for some reason, and we had to crouch down behind the parapet to manage the shots. It all seemed comical and wonderfully illicit. Our sniper-style posture seemed unnecessary, but the Tourist Police officer was wielding a very real AK 47 as well as his smile, and I tend not to argue with policemen armed with a machine gun. The custodians were keen followers of English football, as are most Egyptians, and compared my companion and I to David Beckham and Michael Owen; I fear that their powers of observation were a little compromised by this assertion. The eventual image of the gate was obtained from outside the enclosure wall, after our driver, Azib, kindly made a detour round it to the Karnak end of the avenue of sphinxes which leads to Luxor. It was incredible to see the stumps of these carvings, sometimes used as benches by the local children, jutting out of the dirt of the village through which the avenue ran. Again, a timeless continuity seemed to link the present with the past here.

In Luxor temple, at the other end of the avenue of sphinxes, the debris which was piled deep in Frith's picture has been cleared, although the Mosque of Abu el-Haggag is still perched on top of its mound, the doorway on the temple side high in the air, showing how much has been removed. As we progressed through the temple, for once Egyptians seemed to outnumber tourists, as it was a holiday. Everywhere we went, children ran up to us to say hello, and to ask our names. Some of the girls were keen to have their pictures taken, and there was a real feeling of holiday in the air. How appropriate this was: for the ancient Egyptians, Luxor temple had something of the role of the holiday home of the god Amun-Ra. It was here at the feast of Opet that he was brought from Karnak to spend time rejuvenating himself with his alter ego Amenemope. The festival is seen in reliefs above the hypostyle hall; they date from the reign of Tutankhamun, whose image many of the statues and reliefs reflect. The image reproduced on page 29 (T323014k) has been usurped by the general Horemheb, who became Pharaoh after the death of Tutankhamun's elderly successor Ay.

In ancient times the town we call Luxor was the centre of religious power in the country, and from time to time the centre of political power as well. Frith's images show a rather dilapidated state of affairs, but now it bustles with locals and tourists, with the noise and the smells of the farm mixed with the diesel of the cruise boats moored alongside the Corniche.

In ancient times the west bank was the realm of the dead. The beautiful west was the hoped for destination of any ancient Egyptian. It was the land where the sun set and began its perilous journey through the underworld. The most famous site is the Valley of the Kings, with the tombs of the some of the most powerful men in history. All but one are now empty, as they have been for millennia. Tutankhamun still lies where he was buried in his small tomb in the floor of the valley. Tourists now drift in scorched crocodiles following their guides along very carefully maintained paths. The entrances to the tombs have informative boards outside; how very different to Frith's images of bleak remoteness.

On the other side of the cliff lie the mortuary temples of the kings

ABOVE: THEBES, *A Sculptural Gateway 2004* T323013K

buried in the valley. These were temples dedicated to the memory of the king, and where offerings would be made to preserve the soul of the king in the afterlife. The best preserved is the temple of Rameses III at Medinet Habu (T323002k, T323004k see page 32). It is a little off the main tourist trail, and so it can be explored fairly freely. In Frith's picture (1866e, page 111) the remains of a church can be seen. It was a centre of the Coptic church, and the monastic foundation there was called Djeme. Now all this is cleared, but luckily for modern visitors, the church had plastered over the pagan images, which has had the effect of preserving some of the colour. Our driver Azib was a model of patience and politeness as we rode back and forth across the west bank.

Early one morning we were lucky enough to see the west bank from a balloon, something I feel that my Victorian companion would have enjoyed (T323011k, page 120). It allowed the plans of the temples to be seen and understood in a way that is not always possible from the jumble of stones left on the ground. The quiet of the early morning was breathtaking, and as we rose imperceptibly into the air below the huge red envelope and the barbecue-hot gas burners, small black figures emerged from the houses to mass on the road – not, as it happens, to gaze at the balloon (that must happen every day), but to begin the preparations for a west bank wedding. As we passed over the densely green cultivation, workers in the fields showed a complete lack of interest in our passage.

Back on the ground and on the same day, we returned to the west bank with our driver Azib, and explored the monuments that Frith had photographed all those years ago. The colossi of Memnon seemed unchanged, although now behind them new excavations are exposing parts of the temple of Amenhotep III that only a few years ago were undiscovered. This mortuary temple was huge, dwarfing the Rameseum and the well preserved Medinet Habu, or temple of Rameses III, and further statues are being discovered all the time.

Passing the colossi, we first visited Medinet Habu. This is one of my personal favourite sites; it is well preserved, with much of the original colour still surviving, and it is less crowded than some sites (T323002k, page 32). A bonus on this visit was to walk in the small palace complex next to the building, and to climb the steps to the 'Window of Appearance' and to imagine that you were the ruler. The throne dais (T323004k, page 32) is still in the throne room, and so is the King's personal shower behind it. To stand there made the three thousand-year gap between then and now seem like nothing. There are documents that record the trial of members of the harem of Rameses III, who were accused of plotting to kill him. That he died as a result of this plot is now generally accepted. Here we were, standing in the passages where, in all probability, the conspiracy that killed the king was hatched.

Today the Valley of the Kings is so well known and so much visited by tourists that much of the sense of remoteness of the picture that Frith took (1855, page 33) is lost. The taxi or coach deposits the visitor at a visitor complex, and after tickets have been bought you are ferried up the valley by a small train. We visited in the heat of the day, so there were not so many people there, but the tombs now all have plans at the entrance, and there are well made paths to guide the tourist. In Frith's day, the most exciting find had been of the tomb of Seti I, known as Belzoni's Tomb; it had been discovered by the Italian strong man, who had designed an exhibition of it in London. However, when Frith visited, many of the main sights in the valley had yet to be found. As we had 'visited' the Rameseum from the balloon in the early hours of the morning, we decided to explore some of the less well-known tombs of the nobles, some of which have fantastic relief carving.

Our final stop on our journey was a return to Cairo and an attempt to find some of Frith's mosques. This was difficult, as Cairo has changed more than anywhere else on the journey. It has a population of some 12 million today, and where there was desert in Frith's pictures there is now a very busy by-pass. There is no doubt that the biggest influence on the landscape has been the advent of the motor car. Cairo is carved into sections by wide slashes of tarmac, which channel torrents of cars, lorries, buses and the occasional donkey through the city.

The gate in front of the Citadel that Frith photographed (2813, page 33) shows this change admirably (C711004k, page 155). Now the scene is landscaped and tidy, with access for the visitor. However, the main entrance is now to the south east, where there is more space for a car park. Many of the mosques have undergone renovation, and it is difficult to decide which were the ones photographed by Frith. Not only that, but the buildings around them and the narrow streets made photography difficult.

It was exciting to bustle in some of the back streets with the ever-friendly inhabitants, and the keepers in the mosques were always keen to show us around. The street scenes seemed to be a mixture of old and new.

ABOVE RIGHT: THEBES, *A Painted Lintel, Medinet Habu 1999* T323002K

BELOW RIGHT: THEBES, *The Throne Dais of Rameses III 2004* T323004K

ABOVE LEFT: THEBES, *The Valley of the Tombs of Kings c1857* 1855

BELOW LEFT: CAIRO, *The Citadel Gateway c1857* 2813

ABOVE RIGHT: GEEZEH, (Giza), *The Sphynx and the Great Pyramid c1857* 643

Following in Frith's Footsteps through Modern Egypt

Cars moved slowly through narrow streets where men and boys sat at open-fronted shops, the occasional donkey was urged onwards, and bakers wobbled on bicycles while balancing huge trays of bread on their heads. The smells of spices, diesel and humanity drifted through the windows of the car, but what was most impressive was that in all this chaos there seemed to be little ill-humour, and certainly no road rage; a hand on the horn, a gesture and a smile seemed to get us through.

What impresses the visitor following in Frith's footsteps is the continuity with the past. In rural Egypt, nothing much seems to have changed. But when it comes to people, the distance between the Westerner and the Egyptian seems to have increased, and this perhaps is sad. When the barrier is brought down, the resulting conversations are always interesting, and often entertaining.

We stayed in a modern hotel next to the Giza plateau. From here we were able to walk to the great Old Kingdom monuments. In some ways, the scene seemed to have changed little since Frith's time, or indeed since the time when these surviving wonders of the world were built. However, this appearance is deceptive. When they were first built, these monuments were encased with gleaming white limestone quarried from Tura (Toura), where Francis Frith took photograph 1901E, page 149. The third pyramid would have had a layer of red granite at its base, and it is possible that all the pyramids here had golden caps at their apex. They would also have been surrounded by a complex of temple buildings. It is clear from the photographs that in the 1850s and 1860s the removal of the casing had already taken place (this had been done many hundreds of years before to build medieval Cairo), and that the temples were buried in sand.

The image of the Sphinx (643, page 146) shows clearly how much sand had accumulated. Today the Sphinx has been completely cleared, and over the last ten years restored, with new stone replacing the eroded ancient casing. This is merely the latest stage in a long cycle of burial, excavation, and restoration, which began in the reign of the New Kingdom King Tuthmosis IV (1400–1390BC).

It seems from the place where Frith's photograph was taken that the photographer was standing on part of the buried valley temple of Khafre. This probably looked like a lump of rock protruding from the sand in the mid 19th century. Now it is possible to enter this starkly beautiful temple

ABOVE: GEEZEH (GIZA) PLATEAU, *The Solar Boat of Khufu 2004*
G318002K

and to admire the carefully dressed granite block walls and polished white alabaster floors. You can walk up the sloping ramp which leads to a causeway, which in turn leads to the pyramid temple at the top of the plateau.

Of course, the pyramids are surrounded by the tourists, water-sellers, postcard-sellers, camel-drivers, schoolchildren, and Tourist Police that make up the population of an Egyptian historic site. However, we can visit the Solar Boat museum, something that was denied to Frith, as the boat had not been discovered in his time. The building, rather an eyesore in fact, lies next to the Great Pyramid, above the pit in which the fragments of the boat were found. The size and remarkable preservation of this boat of Khufu make this one of the key sights of the plateau. The ship itself is about the same length of HMS 'Victory' in Portsmouth Harbour, and yet owing to its slender shape it seems much smaller at first (G318002k, page 34, G318003k, page 219). After donning rather unflattering canvas overshoes, visitors are led on shuffling feet around the vessel by the walkways and stairways that allow them to view the ship from all angles. There is some debate about the precise function of the ship. Was it built for the funeral in order to carry Khufu's body across the Nile? Was it used as a royal barge during Khufu's life? Was it built simply to be buried next to the pyramid? Whatever the reason, its survival is remarkable. To see it towering above the pit in which it lay buried for four and a half thousand years is to feel the weight of ages drop away – a familiar feeling for the modern traveller to Egypt.

The pyramids are so huge, so familiar, that it is difficult to stand next to them and to remember that they are the result of man's thought and man's constructive genius. Opening the curtains on a first morning in Cairo to see these great man-made mountains of stone is something of an anticlimax – they simply do not look as if they have ever not been there, so much part of our collective subconscious have they become. You have to think hard to realise that the pyramids were over a thousand years old in the time of Tutankhamun. When the Holy Family fled to Egypt they had stood on the site for over two thousand years; and when Harold was defeated at Hastings, they had pointed at the sky for three and a half thousand years. They seem to be beyond time. That they are the work of man, arising from a bustling work site, is almost beyond belief.

Egypt is a country of immense fascination. Its history is long, and literally near the surface. Francis Frith's records of the country in the mid 19th century and his images of the Holy Land were at the time seen as landmarks in photography. They also subconsciously record the artistic sensibilities of his age, and the attitudes of the west to the east.

It is a great privilege and a pleasure to be able to comment on these impressive images of an Egypt that is now lost to us. The care with which the pictures were taken and developed is impressive, and the record of places that have now changed forever is important both as an archaeological source and as a source of information about the times in which they were created.

After the Timeline, there follows Francis Frith's own account of his Egyptian and Holy Land travels, written as part of a short autobiography, in which he recounts the events of his childhood, his religious and aesthetic development, and his growth into businessman, explorer, photographer, husband and father.

TIMELINE – Egypt and the Modern World

1769	Piranesi's 'Maniere d'Adornare i Cammini', the first book to examine ancient Egyptian design ideas, is published.
1798	Napoleon invades Egypt.
1799	Rosetta Stone discovered.
1800	French surrender in Egypt.
1806	Mohammed Ali becomes the Viceroy in Egypt (1806 – 1849).
1811–12	Egyptian Hall in Piccadilly built.
1815	Belzoni in Egypt. Henry Salt British Consul-General (1815 –1827).
1816–17	Belzoni in Valley of the Kings and Abu Simbel.
1817	Belzoni discovers Seti I tomb.
1820	Drovetti, French Consul-General, active.
	Cleopatra's Needle presented to Britain.
1821	Arrival in Egypt of John Gardiner Wilkinson. James Burton and Robert Hay visit.
1822	Deciphering of hieroglyphs.
	Belzoni's exhibition in Egyptian Hall.
1828	Final part of 'Déscription de l'Egypt' published.
1828–29	Franco-Tuscan expedition led by Champollion.
1831	Original design of the Clifton suspension bridge, showing strong Egyptian motifs.
1835	Egyptian House in Penzance built. First ban on exporting antiquities.
1836	Howard Vyse uses dynamite to blast in to the 3rd Pyramid at Giza.
1837	Andrew Ducrow monument erected at Kensal Green, showing Egyptian influences.
1838	Beginning of David Roberts's expedition to Egypt and the Holy Land.
1839–42	Construction of the Circle of Lebanon and Egyptian Avenue at Highgate Cemetery.
1840	Abney Park Cemetery in Stoke Newington has Egyptian Revival gates designed by Joseph Bonomi.
1842–45	Prussian expedition. Thomas Waghorn begins overland route via Egypt to India.
1843	Owen Jones's 'Views of Egypt' published.
	Pugin produces 'An Apology for the Revival of Christian Architecture in England', a text arguing for the Gothic over the Egyptian style, amongst others.
1847	Opening of new Egyptian galleries at the British Museum.
	George Virtue publishes 'A Christian in Palestine' by Henry Stebbing, with engravings by W H Bartlett.
	Jean-François Portaels produces a series of orientalist paintings, including one of the Kiosk of Trajan.
1851	Mariette in Egypt.
1854	Said Pasha Viceroy of Egypt (1854–1863). Egyptian sculpture gallery opens at British Museum.
	Holman Hunt in Egypt and the Holy Land.

1854	Crystal Palace moves to Sydenham. Egyptian Court designed by Joseph Bonomi and Owen Jones.
1855	Discovery of Harris papyrus in Alexandria.
1856	W H Bartlett's 'The Nile Boat or Glimpses of the Land of Egypt' published.
1857	Owen Jones's 'Grammar of Ornament' published. James Robertson taking photographs in Cairo.
	Francis Frith leaves for Egypt.
1858	The painter William Holman Hunt uses Egyptian design for a chair.
1859	Mariette becomes Director of Antiquities.
	Frith's second visit to Egypt.
1859–60	Frith's third visit to Egypt.
1862	Visit of the Prince of Wales to Egypt (April).
1863	Ismail Pasha Viceroy of Eygpt (1863 – 1879).
1864	Completion of Clifton suspension bridge.
1867	Universal Exhibition in Paris. Edward Poynter's painting 'Israel in Egypt' exhibited.
	Frank Mason Good, Frith's apprentice, in Egypt until 1875.
1869	Opening of Suez Canal. First Thomas Cook tour in Egypt. Viceroy Ishmail Pasha visits Crystal Palace.
1871	First performance of 'Aida'.
1874–5	Construction of Liverpool Street Station with Egyptian-style columns.
1877	Cleopatra's Needle erected on Embankment.
1880	Antonio Beato in Egypt taking photographs of Abu Simbel and Kalabsha.
1882	Egypt occupied by British. Amelia Edwards sets up Egypt Exploration Fund, later to become Egypt Exploration Society.
1883	Liberty's adopt Holman Hunt's Egyptian chair design.
1891	Howard Carter first travels to Egypt.
1898	Francis Frith dies at Cannes.
1912	Discovery of Nefertiti head at Amarna by German expedition.
1914	William Flinders Petrie discovers a hoard of Middle Kingdom jewellery.
1917	Tiffany's kewellery adopts ancient Egyptian motifs.
1922	Discovery of Tutankhamun's tomb.
1923	Duchess of York's (late Queen Mother's) wedding clothing includes a dress in ancient Egyptian style.
1924	Art Deco begins at Paris exhibition. The jeweller Cartier produces the first in a long line of Egyptian-style jewellery.
1927–8	Carreras building in London completed.
1930	Chrysler building in New York shows some Egyptian influence.
1931–2	Hoover building in London.
1937	Agatha Christie in Egypt.
1988	Completion of Sainsbury's Homebase in Kensington.

A True Story – by Francis Frith

I .... determined to travel; the very best thing that a young man of means and leisure can do, if he has not yet found a better destiny. Following my bent towards the romantic and perfected past, rather than to the bustling and immature present, I went East not West. I would begin at the beginning of human history; I would track the Sun back to his rising, and see the lands upon which his first beams fell. I spent two or three years in Asia and Africa, Arabia and Palestine. It would, of course, be easy to fill my book with details of these bewitching wanderings, the memories of which are worth to me, mountains of gold and silver. I treasure them as gems which are inalienable, deathless, perhaps immortal.

My first voyage from Liverpool to Alexandria was a perilous one, in a rolling, wall-sided, nearly new screw-ship, seven times the length of her beam. We had a tremendous gale of wind nearly the whole way, but fair, doing an average with sail and steam of fifteen knots on the flat, and half as much again if you reckon the ups and downs of the tremendous billows. Many a time half the ship's length was covered with a flood of water which she scooped up with her nose in the trough of the wave and tossed backward, when she rose, as by a miracle, quivering in every nerve. When we reached the bar of the harbour, upon which, in fair weather, through a narrow channel, there is only just about depth of water to float a big ship – there was no pilot out! It is pretty certain death to those men if they escape the sea and cannot conceal themselves on shore, after losing a ship. My own experience on a future occasion was only a shade less tragic. I had joined a friend in bringing a little high-pressure steam-launch from England. We too were unable to obtain a pilot to take us round from Alexandria into the Rosetta mouth of the Nile. We therefore attempted the feat ourselves. The weather became rough as we approached the estuary, and we found nothing there but a terrible wall of surf, as far in each direction as the eye could reach. Into this we were at last compelled to steer, apparently to certain death. Very soon the thundering surf leaped upon us. The gauge-glass broken and steam escaped, we were swamped and water-logged! At length, by something very like a miracle, we were dashed, all of us, overboard like so many Jonahs, clinging to the helpless boat, right through the surf to the friendly jaws of the Nile!

Notwithstanding all that I had read and imagined, I was not in the least prepared for the extraordinary and brilliant novelty of the scene that bursts upon the eye on first landing in an eastern port. Alexandria was the greatest 'sensation' that I had ever experienced. Even at this distance of the time, the mere recollection of it is thrilling. There was positively nothing that I had ever seen before, except perhaps a sort of general likeness, in the people, to human form. I had seen what we in England call sunshine, but it was nothing like the vital, almost tangible stuff that made itself part and parcel of the dust and stones and atmosphere of Alexandria. I had read of Arabs and camels, and seen one or two unhappy, silent, isolated expatriations, but they were mere dreams and unrealities beside the genuine, savage aggregates at home. I had been half blinded with dust on English roads, but I now found that hitherto I had no conception of the real meaning of the word Dust. Donkeys and donkey-boys had formerly been, in my eyes, very vulgar and sleepy institutions: not so were they by any means. A scuffle with an army of them, and a triumphant ride, at full gallop, through the narrow, crowded streets to the European Square, upon a chosen specimen named 'John Bright', impelled by a running commentary of the wildest type of Jingoism, whose extravagant and frantic yells and blows I was utterly unable, paralysed as I was with outrageous merriment and laughter, in the least degree to moderate and control. I know not how many muffled-up women, and solemn, well-dressed citizens we jostled and upset; how many fowls and dogs we damaged, in that mad adventure. The fact was that my little attendant imp was so overjoyed that he had secured me for his own personal property during my stay in the city, that he was giving me an ovation. And though still panting with his wild exertions of limb and lung, after he alighted he danced an Arab jig, turned half a dozen somersaults, and then stood on his head in exultant glee!

Alexandria c1785, from an engraving
BY KIND PERMISSION OF TORRIDGE AUCTIONS, BIDEFORD

This vivid orientalism, although it lost of course some of its first exhilaration and novelty, never deserted or failed me. Each morning I awoke to a fresh and joyous consciousness that I was breathing the brighter and freer atmosphere, as it were, of another planet, whose restless fires were burnt out, the smoke and mists exhaled, the cosmogony perfected; intensely, mysteriously interesting and poetic; the present full of calm, contemplative enjoyment, and no dark, anxious future to anticipate. The tide of events and of human life seemed to have come to a tranquil stand; all was enveloped in a glowing, faintly fragrant haze wafted up from the dim regions of the world's fairy-haunted childhood.

It is all very well to study Egyptology and prehistoric history, and to puzzle over hieroglyphics and ethnology at home, but away with them all on the Nile! I would not have the free, unbounded, careless heaven of romance, and the sweet mental repose of such a time invaded and disturbed by any sort of dull, mechanical knowledge about dates and duties and dynasties. I don't want to know whether men or angels or demons built those glowing Temples, and designed and carved those splendidly monstrous and unearthly Beings that link together with such fine sympathy the whole living creation. I am more tempted to worship a crocodile thirty feet long and five hundred or a thousand years old, than to bow down to the God of Calvin; the former seems to me to be the finer and nobler conception of the time.

As to the people: I have spent months, fearing no evil, amongst men whom we call real savages, men whose naked bodies were unctuous with oil, and their matted hair frizzed out to a diameter of a couple of feet, and stuck through with arrows, and who, if they lacked most of the graces of conventional civilisation, are free from most of its conspicuous vices, and whose souls appear to be, if anything, rather more religiously enlightened than is the soul of an average, modern, scientific professor.

Such a spell of exhilaration I enjoyed between the second Cataract of the Nile (the furthest point to which the river is navigable), and the confines of Dongola, through the remotest traces of old-world life, abandoned for centuries to the hyena and the jackal; a spell of feeling entirely incommunicable and inconceivable through any secondary medium. I can still struggle back to the confines of the mental region in which those intensely delightful days were passed, and faintly breathe its enchanted air, but even to myself it is a mere consciousness of something ineffably delicious never to be restored. I had, as it were, smoked the hemp-poison by means of which the Nile-sailor is lifted into the seventh Heaven: the only way to restore the sensation is to smoke it again!

The greatest charm and use of ordinary Nile travelling is that it steeps the mind in a feeling of intense repose. Reclining under a canvas on the cabin top of an old world barge, just such as that upon which Cleopatra lounged, we glide noiselessly up and down the great, silent river, as in a dream. That uneasy craving for books and knowledge which vexes common life, is gone. We do not want to read nor learn, nor even consciously to think. That, if it involved an effort would disturb the peace and display the charm. Our souls are embalmed; our existence is amongst the tombs. We live the life and think the thoughts that the crowds of mummies who surround us, lived and thought.

The placid unfailing sunshine, the deep, dreamy stillness that pervades all nature, and which the creaking of the water-wheel, the monotonous palpitations of the boatman's song, and the cry of the water-bird, only serve to intensify: the looming up at intervals of some vast monument of dim antiquity, of the scarp of a great rock pierced and carved into whole cities of elaborately ornamented and painted habitations of the dead; these are some of the magic influences that crowd upon the mind, through every avenue of sense, and magnetise the most animal nature into clairvoyance of the past.

I spent a summer in Cairo, and its neighbourhood; sweltering in an occasional heat of 108 to 110 degrees Fahrenheit, all through the night, on board my boat, the coolest place I could find: lived for a while at the foot of the great Pyramid, in a house from which, perhaps a thousand years ago, a family which had occupied it for two or three thousand years previously, had been 'ejected' – a tomb! Ate wonderfully concocted dinners deftly served under star-lit trees and verandahs, and beneath the awnings of stately dahabiehs, with the cool night breeze scattering and interweaving at our feet the coloured lights from innumerable fantastic lanterns; listening confidentially while silk-robed Pashas whispered slanders and treason in that gentle well-bred murmur which carries a shaft of irony far more surely and swiftly than any storm of words; fought an awful, midnight battle, to the very point of exhaustion and surrender, with a deadly pack of hungry, wild dogs; spent intervals of six weeks, in alternate fits of storm and calm, bargaining with a mysterious priest who visited me by night, and at length accepted one sixth part of what he first asked, for a splendid, illuminated copy of the Koran, seven hundred years old, in seven huge volumes, written in gold letters an inch high (now in the British Museum; perhaps the finest copy in Europe).

I formed delightful and enduring friendships with English and American travellers, some of whom are since 'known to fame' by their adventures and their writings; saved my Coptic Dragoman, through the medium of our Foreign Office, from utter ruin in the grasp of Mohammedan injustice and bribery; and finally invested in a pair of Arab horses, and bargained with a Sheikh of the Sinai Arabs for six or eight baggage camels and safe conduct during 40 days through Sinai and the 'long desert' to the borders of Palestine.

The transition from water to sand, from the Nile to the Desert, is an easy one. The spirit of the thing is the same, except that the mystery of Nature is somewhat intensified, and the historical associations are less conspicuous. We follow on the spiritualised track of Moses, instead of the material one of the Pharoahs. I first shot quail and wild ducks in the land of Goshen, in places where the sons of Jacob had fed their flocks, and then followed 'the children' over the Desert to Suez, across the Red Sea to the Wells of Moses; to Elim, with its immemorial 'three score and ten palm-trees'; through the Paradise of the Valley of Rephidim, the model Oasis of the world, to the sanctuary of Sinai, and 'the shadow of the great rock', Horeb. Then to the fort of Akaba, where I sat, not with mean persons in the gate, but between the rival Sheikhs of the route to Petra – desert princes got up in true Eastern magnificence, blazing with jewel-hilted swords, and gold-mounted firearms. Their eyes, after some quiet puffing and parley, flashed defiance at each other, and their words were fierce and stubborn – an attitude which they maintained to the last, utterly barring our approach to the land of Edom. So I paid heavily to be escorted by a hitherto untrodden route to Gaza; I fell upon thieves and was robbed; then followed the bargaining for release, the noisy sham-fight amongst the tattered and lean-shanked robbers, the seizing of 'hostages', their escape in the night, carrying off our cooking utensils! A rude mobbing at Gaza, and rescue by the Turkish Effendi, a grandly picturesque and pathetic funeral of a dozen Arabs from the desert brought down to the City and suitably bewailed by a crowd of gaudily-bedizened warriors of their tribe: this was a result of a fight on the very day we had crossed the desert a few miles further south. Another day's march saw us poking about amongst the fine ruins of the cities of the Phoenician Fish-god, Ascalon and Ashdod, and at Gath treading the ghostly courts of Dagon.

Thence my mule scrambled and pattered along the very same stone-paved roads on which of yore King David's mule slipped and scrambled, to the place of his early robber-throne at Hebron, where I prowled lovingly around the jealously lofty walls of the great square Mosque that covers the cave of Machpelah, within which the bones of Abraham and Sarah still (perhaps) rest, and sat in the cool of the day at the door of my tent under the Oak at Mamre, looking not in vain for angel visitors, stealing upon the inner vision, and feasting with me upon spiritual venison. I slept in the fields of Bethlehem, tending imaginary sheep, and heard once more, with mightily augmented sweetness and power, the grand anthem which had rung in my ears from early youth: 'Glad tidings of great joy! Peace on earth to men of good will!'

Nearing Jerusalem, my heart beat high as that of an old Crusader standing up in his stirrups to catch a first glimpse of the queenly city, stretched 'on the side of the North', crowned – but fearfully desolated! Holy and beautiful, but terribly debased and defiled! Nineteen times destroyed, but indestructible! The place of the thrones of David the Pious, Solomon the Magnificent, Manasseh the Idolatrous, Herod the Cruel, Saladin the Infidel, and Godfrey the Chivalrous.

Jerusalem perplexes one, for a while, with the multitude and richness of its associations, and the poverty of some of its modern aspects. These, however, if one has patience with them, grow into harmony. On my last visit I was able in imagination largely to reproduce the past upon the scene, and now, at a long distance alike from the events and the scene, the fusion is complete, and I am able to realise in their local connection, the sacred and stirring and terrible events of its history.

I explored and ransacked the royal city aboveground and underground, pitched my tent over against her walls on this side and that, studied her bulwarks, considered where her palaces and temples stood; lived in a rude, stone-built fortress on the Mount of Olives, blockaded against a band of Arabs of the Jericho Valley – atrocious looking bandits who had recently murdered or carried off a European or two (one of them a lady) for ransom, and who, after reconnoitring me thoroughly, seemed to 'think better of it'. But whilst pretending to escort me, just at the spot where their fathers abused the Good Samaritan's protégé of old, they stole my ammunition, leaving me enough, however, to bag three or four braces of partridges in that wild ravine, on whose rocky sides clings the old monastic den, Mar Saba.

From 'sub-tropical' Jericho and the Valley of the Jordan, and from that strange weird water-crater the Dead Sea, I carried away memories of the dismal square tower whose foundation was laid on the builder's first-born, and its gates set up on his youngest son, and of a ringing chorus of most musical, most melancholy night-singing frogs, whose name was legion: of a rapid, muddy river with densely wooded and ready banks, and of a steaming salt-pan intolerably hot and stifling, whose waters stung and corroded as they dried on the skin, whose shores were ghastly with skeleton-like driftwood, and a few fantastic, distorted shrubs that seemed to be struggling with a curse.

Memory lingers fondly over a hundred points of sacred and romantic interest, and over innumerable incidents of the journey East and North. Bethel, where there are still plenty of stones for pillows, but the ladder has gone back into Heaven, and it is long since the Angels made it their place of alighting: the rich Valley of Shechem with its over-shadows of blessing and cursing, its well of Wells, and its jealously guarded scroll of more than venerable writing: the olive groves around the ruined Roman colonnades and the Christian Church of Samaria. Next the robber-haunted plain of Esdraelon, the great battle-field of Judea, where two or three of the robber-knights, bristling with clumsy arms, dashed their horses breast-high through the weedy tangle, and vainly tried their noisy demands against our quiet, non-resistant, disconcerting composure.

Then over the mountains of Gilboa, to Nazareth, the playground, school, and workshop of the Son of God! Up the woody sides of Tabor and through park-like pastures, studded with Oaks of Bashan, to the hills that overlook the blue waters of Galilee, and the fertile slopes and shores on which stood Chorazin and Bethsaida and Capernaum; to the East, the long range of the Mountains of Moab, and in the North, the snow-capped hill of Hermon:– the finest landscape in Palestine; and blessed is he to who it belongs, 'a thing of beauty and a joy for ever!'

Tiberias whose myriad hosts (of fleas) bit, and no doubt beat, the

A True Story – by Francis Frith

Romans, and whose hot baths restored their composure; the bright waters of the Lake alive with miraculous draughts of fishes, but no Peter to catch them; the cliffs and grottos of the sun-worshippers at Baneas, at whose feet the Jordan rushes out, a full grown river; the wild mountain route beyond, in the granite spurs of Hermon, where a leopard carried off a lamb from a little stone-built ford close to our tent; and at last the dream of my youth, the virgin city of the East, Damascus! amidst whose interminable orchard gardens, heavy with fragrant bloom and glowing fruit, and rippling with thousands of streamlets fresh from the snows of Lebanon, I lost myself for long, luscious, golden days, and serene, blue, starry nights; and mid whose shadowy, aromatic bazaars I lounged and lingered, lazily bargaining for silks and sabres. Musingly I wandered up 'the street called straight', and by the wall against which the basket that held the Apostle scraped nightly. I spluttered over thick coffee-mud in the dingy, bustling café, rested on divans in the marble courtyards soothed by the dashing of fountains and the cooing of doves; blinded my poor eyes with gazing from minarets over miles of those dazzling clay roof flats, from which the whispered secrets are to be proclaimed; confided my fever-stricken groom to the care of a native physician, who sent him a bag of seeds to lie upon, and a bottle of beetles to gaze at, whereupon he recovered; and finally bade a sadly unwilling farewell to the enchanted city, and the gardens of Gull, and wound up the mountains by the headlong course of the Barrada (Abana) over vast fields of snow, to the gigantic ruins of Baalbec, and the Cedar Groves of Lebanon. *[Frith took the only known photographs of the Cedars of Lebanon, before they all fell down in old age.]*

Here were nightingales galore (it was April), and unmistakable cedar scent: patches of snow and wild, stony slopes and ravines. I bought a bottle-gourd full of unparadisically sour wine from a native of Eden, a village nesting in a wooded valley a few miles down the seaward slope, the contents of which bottle were that night dashed, along with the table upon which it stood, into my friend's bed, at which time Boreas from the hills picked up our tent and carried it bodily over the country. We followed, in appropriate night costume, recovering the spoil after a gallant chase.

Down the long slopes of Lebanon my mule-bells jingled, into the streets of Bayrout, and then through interminable orange groves, to Jaffa, whence, nigh to the spot where Simon tanned his hides of Yore, I boarded a French steamer, whose dandified officers paraded the decks of an afternoon in dress-coats and dancing shoes, to Alexandria. Thence to the Bosphorus, Constantinople, Smyrna and 'the Isles of Greece'.

Three times over I slipped away from the damp greenery and the chill pallor of the English climate, from the strain and worry and turmoil of western life to the sunny skies, the warm tranquillity and sweet stagnation of the East. The last time was a feat, and perhaps a folly. Between times I had wisely fallen in love, but the girl was young; I would have one more grand spell of sunshine, and so finally brace up soul and body for the great events of life.

THE PHOTOGRAPHS

with a Commentary
and Francis Frith's Original Notes

The Photographs

EGYPT AND THE NILE

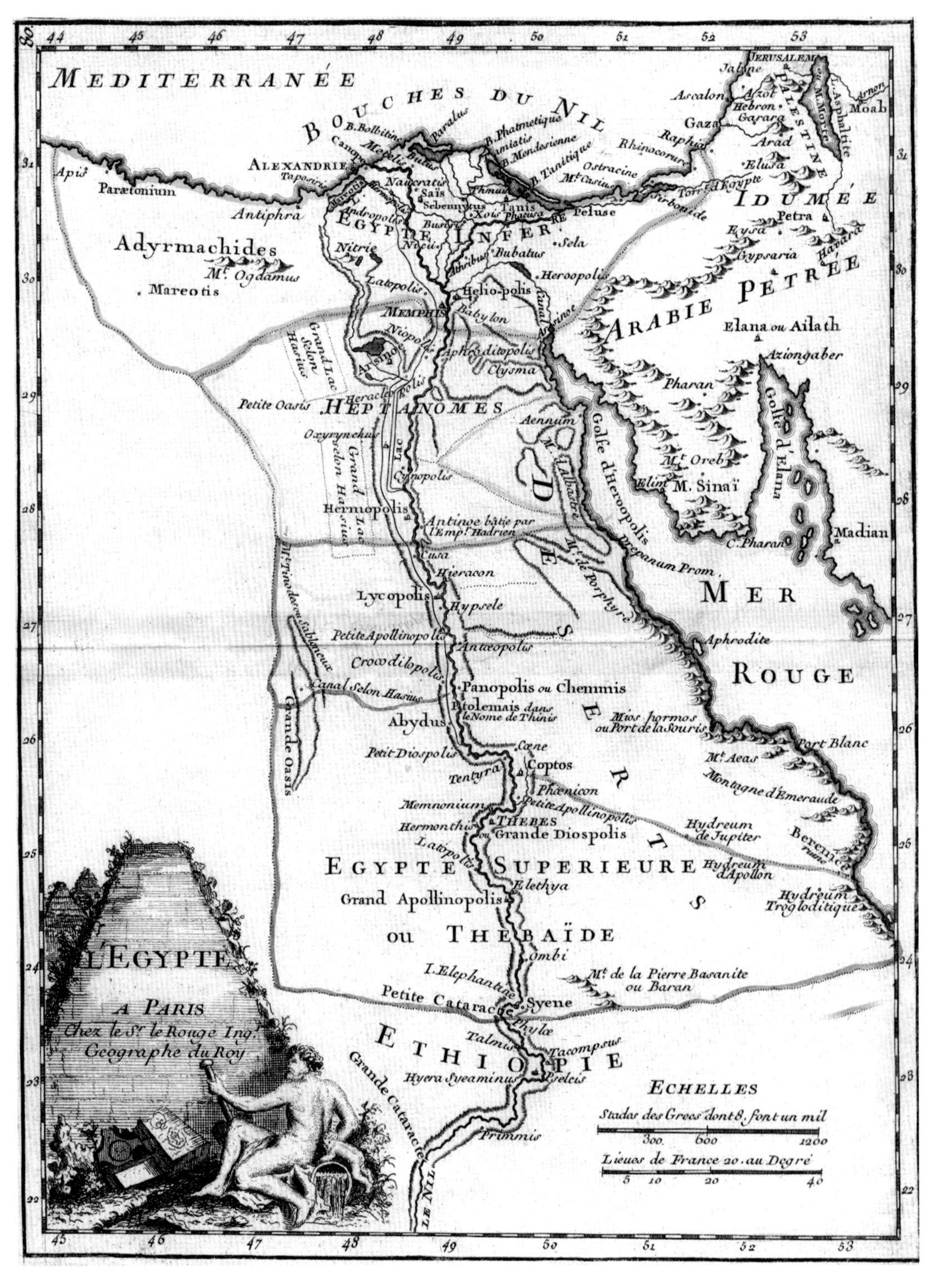

MAP OF EGYPT, AND THE RIVER NILE UP-RIVER TO THE FIRST CATARACT c1756 A001024

ETHIOPIA, *The Remains of the Temple at Amara c1857* 1798E

Although the title of this photograph puts Amara in Ethiopia, in fact Amara lies 155 miles south of Wadi Halfa, well into the Sudan, close to the third cataract of the Nile. The solid bases of this temple are reminiscent of the bases of the hypostyle hall at Karnak, and mark this temple as one dating from the reign of Rameses II. The temple was dedicated to several local gods as well as to the state god of Egypt, Amun. In the time of Rameses there was a flourishing town here.

FRITH'S NOTES ON PHOTOGRAPH 1798

Probably sixty or seventy boat-loads of travellers reach the Second Cataract (Wady Halfah) every season; but very few indeed proceed beyond that point. The Cataract presents the first of a long series of interruptions to the navigation of the river, and the further journey must be performed upon camels as far as the most distant ancient remains, which are found in the 'Island' of Meroe, some five hundred miles south of Wady Halfah. By omitting this journey I do not hesitate to say that the Nile tourist deprives himself of by far the most delightful portion of the trip. Indeed it is my firm conviction that no other district in the world affords such a combination of the true elements of adventure, romance and interest, coupled with the entire absence of serious deprivation or danger. I will therefore commence my narrative of an eighteen days' camel-ride in Ethiopia, with an earnest recommendation to all Nile travellers not to deprive themselves, when it is within their reach, of the present pleasure and life-long recollections of this most enchanting trip.

A sail of forty miles from the temples of Abou Simbel brings us to Wady Halfah, an extensive Nubian village with a resident Turkish official, to whom on my arrival I applied for his assistance in procuring dromedaries, a course which I should not recommend any future traveller to adopt; for I afterwards learned from my camel-men that he pocketed fully half my money. From my experience of these men, I would make my own bargain with them, and trust to their carrying it out faithfully. Leaving my boat at Wady Halfah under the care of an invalid friend, I mounted my dromedary for the south on 8th January 1860. I took with me only my dragoman and the Rias or captain of our boat, an active and obliging little Nubian. Two of the owners of six dromedaries and a boy accompanied us as guides and to take care of the animals. As I purposed travelling beyond a foot's-pace, to which heavily laden camels are restricted, I carried as little luggage as possible – my photographic 'impedimentia' being the chief of it – but my little black operating-tent served to cover me by night. My provision-chest contained biscuit, tea, sugar, and dates,

'I carried as little luggage as possible – my photographic 'impedimentia' being the chief of it – but my little black operating-tent served to cover me by night. My provision-chest contained biscuit, tea, sugar, and dates, with a few little luxuries which were soon exhausted.'

with a few little luxuries which were soon exhausted, and which are by no means a necessity of existence. One of the chief advantages of this trip is, that whilst it gives as complete an experience of desert travelling as one can desire, there is no need to carry water – to submit to an odious decoction of untanned goat-skins. Every evening the traveller may arrange to camp on the banks of the grand old river, which nowhere else inspires him with such an exalted appreciation of its beauty and benevolence as in its course through these tremendous solitudes, which would be dreadful and insupportable without his presence; for, by the consent of all experienced travellers who have tried this 'road', there is nowhere to be found a more savagely grand and gloomy district than the Batn-el-Hadgar, or 'Belly of Stone', as the country for one hundred miles south of the Second Cataract is termed ... On the second day we passed the Cataract and temples of Samneh. The latter contain some interesting sculptures of the Second and Third Thothmes, but are architecturally insignificant. I could not obtain any picturesque point for a photograph.

ETHIOPIA, *The Temple of Soleb c1857* 1838E

'The place is now an utter solitude. The nearest Arab village is a mile or two away. Jackals, large serpents, and musk-cats, occupy the temple.'

FACSIMILE REPRODUCTION OF FRANCIS FRITH'S NOTES TO PHOTOGRAPH 1838 (PREVIOUS PAGE)

THE TEMPLE OF SOLEB, ETHIOPIA.

MY encampment on the western bank of the Nile, nearly opposite the Island of Saye, was on the edge of an extensive sandy plain, sprinkled over with tufts of long Halfah-grass. In crossing it, I observed the tracks of large antelopes; accordingly, at about 4 o'clock on the morning after my arrival, I set out with an old Arab upon our dromedaries in search of the game. We had traversed the plain without success, until, as the day was dawning, we discovered the fresh spoor of an antelope leading away into the desert, and soon perceived that he had been followed by a large beast of prey—doubtless a panther. Shortly we reached the spot where the spring had been made; but the gallant buck had evidently thrown off his assailant, and bounded with incredible leaps into the desert. Knowing well that a hungry panther would never abandon the chase of a fat buck, I at once determined to follow. The spoor of the panther was steadily by the side of the other. He was a heavy animal, and sprang a long leap; but not so long as that of his victim. To make a short story of a long ride—during which I had great difficulty in persuading my Arab to follow—we went for *seven hours* (fully thirty-five miles) fairly into the heart of the desert. My man had tasted nothing that morning, and myself only a small biscuit: of course we had no water. But so determined was I to have venison, if not a panther-skin, that when I could no longer prevail on my Arab to proceed, I left my dromedary in his care, and went forward on foot. The roaring of my camel during this business in all probability saved a life—either mine or the panther's—for I soon came upon the carcase, still warm—a fine ashy-grey buck with both his fore-legs snapped clean in two, and the bones projecting, proving the power of his victor's jaws. He had a splendid pair of twisted horns, 2 feet 6 inches long, which, with his broad fore-hoofs, now adorn my hall. The panther had "disposed of" an entire haunch of the venison, retired some 12 yards, where he had scratched a lair in the sand, and no doubt slept. My weary journey had been cheered by the hope of this result; but, alas! he had been roused by our approach; and although I had not the luck to mark his escape, he had evidently gone off at a pace which must have been very inconvenient after so heavy a meal. On returning to my tent in the evening, I observed that he had prowled during the night all round our encampment—occasionally approaching to within a few yards of where my men lay—perfectly unprotected! We had proof that he was hungry. I cannot imagine why he objected to Arabs and camels! The venison—after nine days at my saddle-bows under a tropical sun—was delicious. The horns and one of the haunches are shown in the foreground of the frontispiece to this volume.

On the sixth day from Wady Halfah I arrived at the Temple of Soleb, the chief object of my journey. It is situated upon an extensive plain, and being visible from a great distance, the approach is very imposing: although, doubtless once the site of an important city (probably *Phthouris*), the place is now an utter solitude. The nearest Arab village is a mile or two away. Jackals, large serpents, and musk-cats, occupy the temple; and from all I could learn, no European traveller had visited it during the previous five years.

It is built of a light-coloured sandstone—at first sight more like limestone—of a quality very inferior to that used in the Egyptian temples. Consequently it is much decayed, and most of the interesting sculpture

THE TEMPLE OF SOLEB, ETHIOPIA.

is almost or entirely obliterated. But enough remains to show that it was built by Amunoph III., the supposed Memnon of the Greeks, and the same who erected the colossal statues on the plain of Thebes. The remains of this magnificent temple are of themselves sufficient to attest that he not only conquered Ethiopia, but maintained his power for a long period.

The entire length of the building was probably from 500 to 600 feet. It was adorned with between 80 and 100 columns. Mr. Hoskins (to whose valuable work on Ethiopia I refer the reader) identified the positions of 84. There were two propylons, one of which is entirely destroyed. The width of the other is 167 feet. The first court had six columns, *ten feet in diameter*. The next apartment was 90 feet by 113 wide, and had 28 columns 19 feet 4 inches in circumference, with the bud-shaped capitals; seven of them remain. The next court was 78 feet long by 113, and had 32 columns, not one of which is standing. Behind these, amidst a stupendous pile of ruin, rises a single pillar with a capital representing branches of the palm-tree—a design which in Lower Egypt is looked upon as of the Ptolemaic era. There were originally 12 columns in this court. The sanctuary is entirely destroyed; but the traces of building extend for another 100 feet; so that, splendid and picturesque as the ruin still is, it evidently gives but a very imperfect idea of the scene, when, *three thousand three hundred years ago*, it stood entire in the midst of a populous and busy city!

South of the third cataract in the Nile lies the important temple of Soleb. The columns are similar to those at the temple of Luxor, and indeed these papyrus bundle columns were built by the same king, Amenhotep III (1390–1352BC). This temple was a large one, dedicated to Amun-Re, although it is interesting in that in common with the later temples of Rameses in this area, it was also dedicated to the deified King Nebmaatre, Lord of Nubia. It has several interesting inscriptions and reliefs illustrating the king's jubilee festival in the 30th year of his reign, the Sed festival, c1360BC. Red granite lions from this temple can be seen in the British Museum.

ETHIOPIA, *Columns at Soleb c1857* 1839E

Frith's Notes to Photograph 1837E

I mentioned our arrival, on the second day (the 9th January), at the temples which overlook the Cataract of Semneh. This is the most remarkable, and I suppose the most formidable to navigation, of the Nile Cataracts. The whole stream passes through a single narrow rocky channel – so narrow that during the spring months a stone may be thrown across. The small remains of the interesting temples crown the rocky heights on each side of the river, where there are also (especially on the west side, by which I ascended, returning on the eastern bank), very extensive ruins of crude brick, which appear to have been military fortifications ...

We had now four days' delightful desert travelling, frequently losing sight of the river, and winding about amongst the stony hills – here and there catching sight of a timid gazelle, too wary to be shot by a mounted hunter. These beautiful creatures frequent the whole of this district on both sides of the river, though not in large numbers. They are proverbially shy and difficult of approach, and can only be shot by skilful stalking. A few covies of long-winged partridges are also met with; the traces of serpents,

Ethiopia, *Ruins of a Christian Church c1857* 1837E

jackals &c., are abundant, and occasionally one sees those of hyenas and wolves. But my experience of the wild life of all real deserts is, that it is extremely scanty. Lizards and beetles, with here and there a solitary raven which preys upon them, are nearly all the life one usually observes in the course of a ten-hours' camel-ride.

The flow of the river throughout the whole of this district is impeded by frequent islands and rocks of granite, which give to the scenery occasional features of much romantic beauty ... On a rock in the desert, by the side of our track, I observed a pistol and a bag of dates, which my guides informed me were placed there by the inhabitants of the nearest village for the use of the Pasha's dromedary post-man. The pistol I found perfectly empty; so I charged it with a good pinch of fine English powder, and filling well up with brown paper, I primed it and replaced it upon the rock. Oftentimes since have I amused myself by imagining the surprise of the worthy government officer when he snapped the trigger with his accustomed bravery. I have even indulged in imaginary pictures of a tawny gentleman prostrate upon the sand, with a post-dromedary vanishing in the distance; and my conscience is not much disturbed by thinking of the official inconvenience which would ensue by the non-delivery of the despatches from Khartoum. An example of the importance of such documents is related by Waddington and Hanbury, who, in the year 1820, were in Ethiopia in the camp of Ismael Pacha, son of Mahommed Ali: – 'The quickest express to the army, from Cairo, came in sixteen days, and brought a letter running thus – "My son! I send you your share of the pears which are just ripe; your brother and myself have found ours very good. Mahommad Ali."'

Near the village of Sukkot above named, and which is famed for the quality of its dates, stands a single column amidst a heap of ruins, marking the site of a town and temple of the time of Amunoph the Third: a few miles further we came in sight of the Island of Saye. The extent and luxuriant appearance of this island led me strongly to hope that I should find important ruins upon it; and upon questioning an Arab whom we met, I was informed that there were four or five splendid temple-ruins upon the island, brilliantly painted red or green! The latter part of the story made me entirely distrust the whole; but observing a boat on the opposite side – the only one we had seen since leaving Wady Halfah – we succeeded in obtaining it, and made in it a perilous voyage to the island – baling out the water merrily all the way to keep our barque afloat – for she was built of rough round logs of acacia most questionably strung together. On landing, my dragoman seized the first donkey that presented itself, and mounting me thereupon, we proceeded with a numerous train of natives in quest of the five temple-ruins. After a ride of two hours into the interior, we arrived at the site which I have copied, evidently the ruins of a Christian Church – rude granite columns with capitals of the Greek Cross – an interesting memorial of the early establishment of our religion in these remote parts of the earth. A remarkable mountain with a flat table-top is seen in the distance. This is Gebel Ollaky, situated in the eastern desert on the other side the Nile.

ETHIOPIA, *An Encampment c1857* 1800E

'There is a wonderful air of repose and placid dignity about these gigantic features, which strikes one as the most or only suitable expression for the task in which they are engaged ... unmoved not simply during thousands of years, but in all human probability through all time!'

The kingdoms of Nubia began to be converted to Christianity during the 6th century, some two hundred years after the edict of Theodosius (AD 390) began to close the pagan temples. The impetus for change came from two sources: the Byzantine Empire, who sent out emissaries with a view to converting the south (the first of these was led by an Egyptian monk named Julian), and Egypt, whose wandering monks worked with and influenced the people of Nubia. Frith's view of the columns of a church (1837E, page 52) is of the remains at Sai, which lie on an island south of the Nile's third cataract at Wadi Halfa (it lies in the Sudan, although Frith calls it Ethiopia). The remoteness of the spot had a strong effect on Francis Frith, and so did the finding of a Christian church in such a remote place: he talks of 'a flood of mental and physical exhilaration'. This remoteness can be sensed in the image of the encampment (1800E, page 54), where we see camels and people huddled around the base of a doum palm, presumably for shade. To date no excavations of the church at Sai have been carried out.

FRITH'S NOTES TO PHOTOGRAPH 1793E *(overleaf)*

This is a front view of one of the four colossal figures which adorn the facade of the great temple. It is the lowest of the four, i.e. the one nearest the river. I chose it as being the least encumbered with sand. From its immense height, the features are somewhat foreshortened and distorted.

Perhaps a more correct appreciation of the face is obtained in the next view, which shows it in profile. They were all representations, and probably portraits of Rameses the Second, who reigned about 1350 years B.C. They are carved from the living rock, are seated on thrones, and are executed in the very best style of Egyptian art. The beauty of the countenances, or at any rate, the perfect adaptation of expression to their situation and purpose, has been remarked and admitted by all travellers. There is a wonderful air of repose and placid dignity about these gigantic features, which strikes one as the most or only suitable expression for the task in which they are engaged, viz., of watching in that desert solitude, unmoved not simply during thousands of years, but in all human probability through all time!

The total height of the figures is about 60 feet. According to Sir G. Wilkinson some of their dimensions are – 'the ear, 3 feet 5 inches; forefinger, i.e., to the fork of the middle finger, 3 feet; from inner side of the elbow-joint to end of the middle finger, 15 feet.' The general effect of their proportions, as compared with that of the human figure, is shown in the picture by the introduction of two

NUBIA, *A Colossal Figure at Abou Simbel c1857* 1793E

Arabs upon the lap of the statue, which is 25 feet 4 inches across the shoulders.

Irby and Mangles state that these figures were uncovered by their party only as far as the breast. Many years afterwards the two lower ones were excavated to the base by Mr. Hay, but the sand is again encroaching, and it will require the continued efforts of travellers to keep the temple open.

On the sides and on the front-corners of the thrones are female figures (the head of one is visible in my Photograph), which are conjectured to represent the wives and children of the monarch. And this reminds me that Lepsius professes to have recovered from the monuments the following particulars of his domestic history. He informs us that his progeny consisted of one hundred and sixty-two children.

Before his investigations he tells us only twenty-five sons and ten daughters of this great king were known; and finally, 'that he did not take the two legitimate wives which appear on this monument simulataneously, but the one after the death of the other!' – so minute is the autobiography which this man of 3200 years ago has left for the edification of the 'ends of the earth!' I consider that these portraits are little less than self-deification on the part of the monarch who, in the interior, is actually represented as worshipping himself, while at Gerf Hossayn, another rock-temple of his own construction, he is even called 'Ruler of the Gods'. From some remaining traces, it seems probable that the whole of this exterior was originally covered with stucco and painted.

NUBIA, *The Facade of the Great Temple at Abou Simbel from the East c1857* 1795E

'As he watches their movements, a great horror seizes him (in spite of his antiquarian enthusiasm) at the idea of exchanging his luxurious cushions for the heavy climb up the steep evasive sand-slope, with the thermometer at 130 degrees.'

Frith's Notes to Photograph 1795E
(previous page)

The subterraneous works of the ancient Egyptians, such as the rock temples of Nubia and the tombs of Thebes and of Lower Egypt, are quite as wonderful as the most celebrated of their structures, not excepting even the temples of Luxor and Philae.

The great rock temple of Abou Simnel, the facade of which is represented in the Photograph, is situated about forty miles to the north of the Second Cataract, and is the most southerly of the ancient monuments of Egypt usually visted by Europeans; but they are to be found extending as far south as Dongola, 1300 miles from the mouth of the Nile.

I am sure that to have stood – even thus far towards Central Africa – and to have gazed by the intense light of a Nubian sun upon the facade of this glorious temple, the broad river flowing at its base, the palm groves beyond, and the deep yellow desert hills which close the distance, must have enriched the mind of everyone who has beheld the scene, and is possessed of a spark of imagination, with images of mingled beauty and grandeur, and romance, which will occasionally haunt through life his happiest and most contemplative moments. The stillness and desolation of the very desert from which these noble evidences of a populous antiquity are but half disentombed, will have heightened the mysterious sublimity of their effect upon the mind; and perhaps the traveller will often refer to the features of the figures of the facade as the only perfect combination of colossal size with ideal bauty which he ever beheld.

The temple is sculptured in the face of a sandstone rock, which runs sheer down to the river; and here the traveller who arrives 'in season' usually finds a long line of 'dahibiehs', showing an abundance of gaudy flags and pennants, and occasionally saluting with the customary 'complement' of gunpowder the arrival or departure of a comrade.

The new arrival, with the help of his opera-glass, observes Brown, Jones and Robinson, with a party of ladies (they have all been married since their continental tour) toiling through the deep sand to the entrance of the temple; also Lord Henry —, and two other gentlemen, whom he remembers to have seen on the shady side of Pall Mall, looking much cooler than they do at present; and, as he watches their movements, a great horror seizes him (in spite of his antiquarian enthusiasm) at the idea of exchanging his luxurious cushions for the heavy climb up the steep evasive sand-slope, with the thermometer at

130 degrees. However, the effort must be made; he goes ashore, and arriving at the temple, reduces himself to a sedentary position, and – emboldened by the example of the ladies – executes a glissade through the narrow entrance, excavated by Belzoni, Irby and Mangles, in the year 1817, into the great hall of the temple, where the scanty glimmering of day-light, added to that of his candle, reveals to him the eight colossal Osiridae figures, with arms folded upon their breasts, and the beautiful sculptures wich adorn the walls. 'The Osiridae figures', says Sir G. Wilkinson, 'are 117 feet 8 inches high, without the cap and pedestal'. To this grand hall succeeds a second, with four square pillars supporting its roof; a corridor and an 'adytum', with two side chambers. Eight other rooms open on the grand hall. The total depth of the excavation is about 200 feet. The temple is of the time of Rameses II (about 1400 years B.C.), of whom the colossal figures of the facade are probably portraits. There were originally four of these, but the one on the left of the entrance has fallen away from the face of the rock, and the uppermost on the right is buried to the chin in the drifted sand. These figures are about 60 feet high; the ears measure 3 feet 5 inches. The principal sculptures of the interior are historical subjects relating to the conquests of its founder, and extend from the first to the thirty-fifth year of his reign.

The figure to be seen in 1794E (right) is the image of the sun god Re-Horakhty, a falcon headed god, who was associated with the rising sun. Indeed, this figure is looking towards the east.

NUBIA, *The Entrance to the Great Temple c1857* 1794E

'They arrived upon the spot on the 4th of July, 1817, after desperate struggles with a mutinous crew, and a murderous dragoman. Those who have not experienced the heat of a tropical sun at midsummer, can form but a faint idea of the credit which is due to the party for their perseverance in the labours.'

Frith's Notes to Photograph 1794E

(previous page)

As might be anticipated, and as was predicted by its discoverer, Burkhart, in 1813, the entrance to the great temple is in the centre of the facade. After speaking of the heads of the colossi, he says – 'On the wall of the rock, in the centre of the four statues, is a figure of the hawk-headed Osiris surmounted by a globe, beneath which I suspect, could the sand be cleared away, a vast temple would be discovered'. The figure, however, is not Osiris, but Re, to whom the temple was dedicated. This same idol is one of the four sitting figures in the sanctuary. On each side of him (in our view) the king is offering a figure of Truth. The object on the extreme right of the view is the shoulder and first joint of the arm of one of the four colossi. It is supported by masonry, whilst that on the opposite side of the doorway has fallen.

Burkhart communicated his discovery to Belzoni, and in the year 1817 he and Mr. Beechey proceeded up the Nile for the purpose of opening the temple. At Philae they had the good fortune to be joined by those enterprising travellers, Captains Irby and Mangles, and few narratives of this sort are so interesting as is their account of the progress of their undertaking. In view of the results of their labours, I cannot do better than epitomize this narrative. It should be understood that the Nubian chiefs were then virtually independent rulers; very few travellers had penetrated so far south, and without the utmost skill and firmness in in their intercourse with these savages, the party could not hope to remain so long in one place, as was necessary for the success of their enterprise, without the greatest danger of serious molestation. They arrived upon the spot on the 4th of July, 1817, after desperate struggles with a mutinous crew, and a murderous dragoman. Those who have not experienced the heat of a tropical sun at midsummer, can form but a faint idea of the credit which is due to the party for their perseverance in the labours which we are about to relate. Seven days were lost in negotiations with the two chiefs, whose good-will it was necessary to secure – large presents were given them, and promises on their part were repeatedly made and broken – until at length on the 11th the labour was commenced by fifty men, who worked very badly, the burden of their song being, 'that it was Christian money they were working for – that Christian money was very good, and that they would get as much of it as they could'. A bargain was then made with the chiefs to open the temple for a stipulated sum. They persevered in this mind but one day, although half the sum was paid down. The Muslem fast of Ramadan was approaching, during which it would be impossible to induce the Arabs to remain; but several days intervened, spent in most provoking quibbles, and attempts at extortion, by the chiefs. They then took themselves off to a distant part of the country – giving their consent that the party should be allowed to do the work themselves – on condition that due notice should be given to the chiefs when the door was about to be uncovered, and that they should share the gold found in the interior! 'On the 16th', says the Journal, 'we stripped to the waist and commenced, six in number, including the Greek servant and the janizary; we resolved to work, and regularly persevered from 3 o'clock till dark in the evenings, and from the very first dawning of the day till nine in the mornings.' This plan was pursued, with occasional help from the crew, and frequent interruptions from the natives, who often threatened personal violence, during fifteen days, the thermometer ranging from 112 to 116 degrees Fahr. in the shade. The temple was entered on the 1st of August, 50 feet of sand having been removed from the doorway. It had probably been closed during a period of 3000 years!

NUBIA, *Abou Simbel from the West c1857* 1796E

ABOVE: NUBIA, *Abou (Abu) Simbel 1997* N209002K
BELOW: NUBIA, *Temple of Rameses II, Abou (Abu) Simbel 2004* N209011K
RIGHT: NUBIA, *Abou (Abu) Simbel 2004* N209001K

When Frith took the photographs of Rameses II's temple at Abu Simbel it was in its original position. Since then it has been cut away from the rock face, dismantled, and moved to a new, higher location to avoid the rising waters of Lake Nasser.

The temple was originally dedicated to the three gods Amun-Re, Horus of Mehu, and Ptah, as well as the deified Rameses II (1279–1213BC). The carved inscriptions mentioned by Frith show Rameses fighting against the Hittites at the battle of Kadesh. This became an iconic image of victory for Rameses, although in reality the battle seems to have ended in stalemate and to have been followed by a peace treaty which was equitable to both sides. The first expedition by westerners to the interior of the temple was led by Belzoni, as Frith says in his accurate and detailed commentary on the scene. The commentary to print 1795E gives an amusing account of the arrival of tourists at the famous site (see page 58). Frith manages a detached observation of his fellow travellers, which counters the rather jingoistic accounts of tourism in Egypt to be found in the popular papers of the time. For instance, the Illustrated London News of 25 April 1857 reported that 'when you want the man you clap your hands; Englishmen out of England being the merriest dogs in existence, and with as many as 300 people clapping their hands at once, the poor darkies did not know where to run!' Today the scene is as impressive, though in a less romantic way. The walk through the huge concrete dome behind the reconstituted rock face onto which the temple was rebuilt adds a dimension that Frith could not have imagined, and of which Rameses himself would have been proud.

ABOVE: NUBIA, *Abou (Abu) Simbel, Re-Horakhty 2004* N209003K

NUBIA, *The Façade of the Smaller Temple c1857* 1797

NUBIA, *The Façade of the Smaller Temple c1857* 1797 (PREVIOUS PAGE)

Like the larger, better-known temple, this one, dedicated to Hathor and the deified wife of Rameses, (Nefertari in the form of Isis-Hathor), has been moved to a higher position to escape the rising waters of Lake Nasser. The face of the temple cut into the rock is in the form of a pylon gate flanked by images of the king, and on a smaller scale by images of his wife, whose temple this is. The two temples, sited on the southern boundary of ancient Egypt, made a political statement: they proclaimed the might of the royal house of Egypt to the Nubian rulers of 'Vile Kush' to the south, who in Egyptian imagery were normally shown bound or being struck by the king. On Tutankhamun's footstool, for instance, Nubians and other enemies of Egypt are bound, ready to be trodden on by the king.

IBRAM, *The Traveller's Boat 1857* 647E (OVERLEAF)

The earliest evidence of occupation at Qasr Ibrim dates from the early New Kingdom. From that date it has had a colourful history of occupation. A temple to Isis was built here by the Nubian 25th dynasty King Tarhaqa (690–664BC), and was one of the last working temples in Egypt. A cathedral stood on the site until the 10th century. It was eventually taken by the Ottomans in the 16th century, who converted the church into a mosque. It was destroyed in 1812 after having been used as a fort by the Mamelukes.

When Frith visited the site, it was high on a rocky promontory dominating this reach of the Nile. Today it is a rather less imposing island; the outer areas of the ruin visible in the upper left middle distance have been submerged under Lake Nasser. In the foreground of the picture is the boat that Frith used to navigate the Nile. The cabin at the rear with the canopy over it reminds us of the cabin of the solar boat of Khufu at Giza.

IBRIM, *Qasr Ibrim 2004* I72001K

IBRIM, *The Traveller's Boat c1857* 647E

NUBIA, *Colossi and Sphinx at Wady Saboua c1857* 1801 (DETAIL)

At the original site of el-Saboua there were two pharaonic temples, one built by Amenhotep III and the other by Rameses II. As the valley flooded, only the one built by Rameses survived. This was the one that Frith saw, and whose causeway entrance he photographed.

To the left of the picture the sand has clearly covered the temple proper, and only two statues of the king and two sphinxes are clearly visible. To the left of the pair in the foreground we can see the partly covered back of another sphinx.

Now the whole temple complex can be visited. It is dedicated to a Nubian form of the sun god Re-Horakhty, meaning 'Re of the two horizons'. The statues of the king in the temple are in a rounded local style, quite different to the style further north.

NUBIA, *Wady (Wadi) Saboua 2004* N209006K

Frith's Notes to Photograph 1801

(previous page)

At Korosko, near Wady Saboua, I found one or two of the Pasha's steamers, and a considerable body of troops stationed. The Pasha had gone overland from Korosko to Khartoum, to meet Theodosius, the new 'Emperor' of Abyssinia – an energetic and spirited man, who after uniting under his power the petty hostile kingdoms into which this district has for centuries been divided, had so far threatened the southern provinces of Egypt, as to induce Said Pasha to meet him in conference, backed by about ten thousand soldiers.

These potentates, as I afterwards learned, effected a meeting, and matters were understood to be amicably arranged. The Patriarch of the Coptic Church, being also the head of the Established Church of Abyssinia, was subsequetly sent by Said Pasha as an ambassador to the court of Theodosius, who received him with much apparent distrust, and made a sort of state prisoner of him, keeping him strictly guarded in his own immediate train. Then, suddenly summoning all his chief men, he demanded of his prisoner, that if he were the Patriarch he professed to be, he should crown the Emperor, there and then, as the deputed head of his church in Abyssinia; thus adding, by a stroke of wily policy worthy of a more civilised monarch, a most powerful support to his newly-acquired temporal dominion; for the reverence of the eastern churches for their supposed spiritual leaders is very great. The Coptic Patriarch, who is himself an unusually shrewd, intelligent, artful man, and a progressionist withal, was detained for many months at the court of Theodosius, without being able even to communicate with his anxious friends at Cairo. But he has at length been allowed to return, with a fund of anecdote and information as to the social and political condition of a country which bids fair, under the rule of Theodosius, to rise in the scale of nations almost as strangely and as rapidly as Egypt did under the able government of Mahmmed Ali.

At Korosko, the Nile, whose course is almost uniformly south, takes a sudden bend to the north-west, and in this bend, on the northern bank, are the temples of Amada and Wady Saboua. The former did not afford me a picture – it is exceedingly plain externally, and almost entirely buried by the drifted sand. Its interior, however, contains some beautiful sculpture of the very early age of Osirtasin III, consequently more than 3500 years old. Even the colours are quite fresh in some places, having been preserved by the plastering of mud with which the early Christians concealed the emblems of idolatry.

Wady Saboua is thus described by Sir G. Wilkinson: – 'Saboua, so called from the "lions" (androsphynxes) of the dromos, is of the early time of Rameses the Great. It is all built of sandstone, with the exception of the adytum, which is excavated in the rock. The dromos was adorned with eight sphynxes on either side, and terminated by two statues with sculptured stelae at their back: to this succeeded the two pyramidal towers of the propylon; the area, with eight Osiridae figures attached to the pillars supporting the architraves and roofs of the lateral corridors; and the interior chambers, which are now closed by the drifted sand. Amunre and Re were the chief deities, and from the worship of the god of Thebes, the town bore the same name as that city – Amunei, or the abode of Amun.'

The reader will conjecture that the desolate figures which form my picture are the two statues which terminated the dromos, and some of the mutilated bodies of the androsphynxes. The pylon of the temple is rude, and very much dilapidated; and it appeared to me that these figures were most impressive, standing alone, as I have represented them, amidst the sultry stillness of the desert, whose remorseless sand-waves are gradually stealing round, and engulfing them.

'The pylon of the temple is rude, and very much dilapidated; and it appeared to me that these figures were most impressive, standing alone, as I have represented them, amidst the sultry stillness of the desert, whose remorseless sand-waves are gradually stealing round, and engulfing them.'

ABOVE: NUBIA, *Wady Kardassy 2004* N209009K

LEFT: NUBIA, *The Colossus of Rameses II, Wady (Wadi) Saboua 2004* N209007K

NUBIA, *The Temple of Wady Kardassy c1857* 1809

'And here stands the "dark ladie" whom we sought, for ever overlooking that sweet silent scene, like an Eve who has not lost her paradise – created young, and still as young as ever; more like a maiden upon whom the last grace of womanhood is not yet bestowed, than one whose day is passed.'

Frith's Notes to Photograph 1809

(opposite)

Here is a bonnie little ruin! It has no history. no lineage, no armorial bearings; – it is like the pretty milk-girl, whose 'face was her fortune', except that, unlike her, it boasts a plurality of faces – heads of Isis, with long rectangular ears, adorning each square of the lower capitals.

Now, it would be rather a relief to contemplate for once an Egyptian temple without sculpture; but then, thou must resign thyself for this time to romance – go desperately in love with my Nubian beauty, dismiss learning and conjecture, and throw thyself at her feet in a transport of dreamy blissful admiration!

It is very early morning: the sun of Nubia has just risen and is painting golden lines upon the eastern edges of the landscape, and rich deep shadows (albeit transparent) upon the temple basements, and underneath the opposite shore of the silent solemn river; and here stands the 'dark ladie' whom we sought, for ever overlooking that sweet silent scene, like an Eve who has not lost her paradise – created young, and still as young as ever; more like a maiden upon whom the last grace of womanhood is not yet bestowed, than one whose day is passed.

And this, indeed, is the aspect of many a Nile ruin; for although some were never really completed, yet many shattered ones, from the wonderful freshness of the stone, look merely unfinished. It seems as though the works had been stopped last year for want of funds, and that the Government might now, without astonishing anyone, put the men 'on' again.

I wonder if some benign governor will one day perfect any of these structures, according to their original designs! Would there be any harm in such a proceeding? Or had they best remain just as the Fates have willed them – genuine, though dreadfully mutilated relics of the days of 3000 years ago?

NUBIA, *Greek Tablets at Wady Kardassy c1857* 1811

Frith's Notes to Photograph 1803

When one enters a stupendous temple whose foundations were laid three thousand years ago, and after passing from hall to hall and from chamber to chamber, whose walls are all vocal with the quaint language of forgotten time, an apartment is reached in which the artist's hand seems but that instant to have laid aside his chalk – how powerful and strange is the appreciation, as it were, of the momentary lapse of ages! How difficult to realize the fact, that two thousand years ago that hand was stayed, and that work will never be resumed!

NUBIA, *The Temple of Maharraka c1857* 1803

NUBIA, *The Temple of Maharraka 2004* N209004K

These remarks are suggested by the subject of my present picture. 'The Temple of Maharraka', whichis situated about eighty miles above Assouan, is perhaps the most strikingly modern and unfinished-looking ruin in Egypt. The capitals of the columns are for the most part in the block, showing that even in the Roman times these, and all similar elaborate embellishments, were sculptured from the rough block, after it had been put into place. At Medinet Haboo, I observed an immense outer pylon wall, which had been built up of rough stones, the bead at the angle and a little of the surface only having been smoothed.

NUBIA, *The Temple of Dabod c1857* 1812E

'There is now, as is almost invariably the case in the neighbourhood of a temple, a small Arab village at Dabod, from one of whose native sportsmen I purchased the skin of a hyena, and heard more wonderful stories of his adventures in pursuit of wild beasts than my readers would be likely to credit.'

FACSIMILE REPRODUCTION OF FRANCIS FRITH'S NOTES TO PHOTOGRAPH 1812E (OPPOSITE)

THE TEMPLE OF DABOD.

BEYOND Philæ, at the distance of eight miles, are the ruins of the temple of Dabod. The site is probably that of the *Parembole* of Antoninus. Here we begin to meet with the names of the monarchs of Ethiopia. Dabod appears to have been built by a king named Ashar-Amun, or Atar-Amun, who was the successor of Ergamun, the founder of the temple of Dakkeh, and the contemporary of Ptolemy Philadelphus. The temple is grievously dilapidated: between the periods of my first and second visits a large portion of it had fallen. There are still three pylon gateways standing: the first is not shown in the view. The main building consists of a portico with four columns, connected by screens, a central chamber with a smaller one on each side, and a staircase which led to the upper apartments. Then follow another central and two other side chambers, and the adytum, which does not contain any sculpture, but monoliths within it bear the names of Physcon and Cleopatra. The name of the founder, Ashur-Amun, is found in one of the front chambers; he is designated "the Everlasting," and "the beloved of Isis," to whom with Osiris, and their son Horus, the temple was dedicated. Most of the sculptures were added in Roman times, chiefly by Augustus and Tiberius, but the building was left in an unfinished state, which is also the case with a large proportion of the Roman ruins in Nubia.

When Mr. Hamilton visited Dabod, he found on the front of the central pylon a Greek inscription, which he translated thus—"For the welfare of King Ptolemy and Queen Cleopatra (the sister) and wife, gods Philometores, to Isis and the contemplar gods . . . . ." The three pylons are not placed at equal distances. The first was built into the wall of circuit, part of which remains. Upon the portico is a sculpture representing the gods Thoth and Hor-Hat, engaged in pouring alternate emblems of life and purity over Tiberius; alluding, says Sir Gardner Wilkinson, to the ceremony of anointing him king. The only other remains here are those of a stone quay and staircase leading down to the river. There is now, as is almost invariably the case in the neighbourhood of a temple, a small Arab village at Dabod, from one of whose native sportsmen I purchased the skin of a hyena, and heard more wonderful stories of his adventures in pursuit of wild beasts than my readers would be likely to credit.

NUBIA, *The Temple of Dakkeh c1857* 1802

Today the Nubian temples are visited from a Nubian sea cruise ship. The Rameside temple from Wadi Saboua stands at the edge of Lake Nasser, and today it has been cleared of the sand that seems to engulf it in Frith's image. It was dedicated to Amun, the deified Rameses II, and Re-Horakhty. The temple was moved in the 1960s to its present location to escape the rising Lake Nasser. The avenue of sphinxes and the exterior of the temple are an impressive sight in the desolation of the Sahara, although the carving in the temple itself is at times rather crude.

The Temple of Dakkeh has been re-erected not far from the new site of the Rameside temple, and on its elevated location it makes an impressive picture from the lake. It was begun by Arkamani, one of the kings of Meroë, a kingdom in what is now the Sudan, in about 220BC. He, like all of these kings, was Nubian by birth. The temple was completed in the Ptolemaic period, and most of the decoration visible today is of this time. It is also notable for the Victorian travellers' graffiti, showing that it was visited before Frith saw the monument himself.

The temple of Maharraka has been rebuilt too, and now stands just to the south of Dakkeh temple. It dates from Roman times, and it is completely changed since the time that Francis Frith took his picture. In the 1857 photograph (see page 73) we see a tumble of blocks in front of the pillared hall. Today, the blocks have been rebuilt around the hall, and from the outside the temple has a stark and austere exterior. Inside, it is clear that the temple was unfinished because of the lack of carved reliefs and the undecorated pillar capitals.

The area of southern Egypt and northern Sudan known as Nubia owes its name to the ancient Egyptian word for gold, 'nub'. For the kings of Egypt, this area with its gold mines was one of the main sources of their wealth. It also periodically caused military trouble for the pharaohs, and a figure of a bound Nubian was a regular feature of the iconography depicting the power of the king – for example, one of Tutankhamun's walking sticks uses a bound Nubian for the handle. The reason for the large number of temples here could be that the pharaohs wanted to demonstrate their power in this sometimes unstable area. With the building of the high dam at Aswan, the Nile valley above the first cataract has been flooded, and the temples are threatened with destruction. However, a conservation programme funded by UNESCO saved many during the 1960s and 1970s, and they can be seen today on the shores of Lake Nasser.

NUBIA, *The Temple of Dakkeh 2004* N209005K

NUBIA, *The Temple of Gerf Hossayn c1857* 1806E

The temple in 1806E (previous page) is now covered by the waters of Lake Nasser. It is built in a similar style to the temple at Abu Simbel, but it is smaller. This rock cut temple from the time of Rameses II was dedicated to the worship of Ptah, Ptah-Tenen, Hathor, and the deified Rameses. Frith's account of his stay here gives us an insight into the problems of operating in such a hot environment. He talks of working on his images by candlelight in the interior of the temple; the floor was covered in foul-smelling dust, almost certainly the droppings from the bats that he also describes. He was shown the temple by 'a host of importunate guides'. This phenomenon of 'guides' appearing as if from nowhere to show the visitor around is familiar to visitors to Egypt today.

'Our party was observed by the Arabs of the village as we scrambled over the hot glaring rocks towards the ruin, and presently, nolens-volens, we were escorted by a host of half-naked importunate "guides", carrying torches of dried palm-leaves.'

Frith's Notes to Photograph 1806E *(page 78)*

About sixty-six miles above the First Cataract, at a considerable elevation above the plain, upon a rude platform excavated from the limestone rock, stands the temple, the area and portico of which I gave in the present illustration. The commanding position of this ruin, the bold and massive character of its sculptured columns, and above all, the aspect of extreme antiquity which its design and time-worn condition impart – all render a visit to Gerf Hossayn of great interest to the Nile traveller. It is a scene which takes hold of the mind, and is not easily effaced. With the exception of the portico, it is entirely an unexcavated temple, of the time of Rameses the Great.

At the upper end of the adytum are several sitting figures in high relief. In the great hall there are also eight niches, containing similar figures. There are several chambers with a variety of emblematic sculpture. The total depth of the excavation is about 130 feet. Sir G. Wilkinson says: – 'The Osiridae figures in the hall are very badly executed, ill according with the sculpture of the second Rameses; nor are the statues of the sanctuary of a style worthy of that era. The deity of the adjoining town (the ancient Tutzis) was Pthah – "The Creator and Lord of Truth", to whom the dedications are inscribed.'

Our party was observed by the Arabs of the village as we scrambled over the hot glaring rocks towards the ruin, and presently, nolens-volens, we were escorted by a host of half-naked importunate 'guides', carrying torches of dried palm-leaves. These, as we entered the temple, they prepared to light, but by the time they were in full smoke, we had finished our hasty inspection of the interior.

It was truly amusing to see the blank astonishment of the Arabs – standing in the doorway with their torches – when, instead of the minute examination of the interior sculptures, in which they had been accustomed to 'assist' travellers, we proceeded rapidly and silently to arrange and point the camera towards them from the outer area. Silently and rapidly they too 'went about their business'.

I prepared my pictures by candle-light in one of the interior chambers of the temple. It was a most unpleasant apartment – the hole in which I worked. The floor was covered to the depth of several inches with an impalpable, ill-flavoured dust, which rose in clouds as we moved; from the roof were suspended groups of fetid bats – the most offensively smelling creatures in existence; in some tombs the odour which they emit is so powerful as to render the place 'impossible'.

Add to all this, that the Arabs seem to have been industriously smoking this wretched temple from time immemorial, even, in places, to the complete effacement of the sculptures upon the walls – and you have a picture of the interior of Gerf Hossayn: but without, besides this quaint old portico, are the sun and sky of Nubia, and the groves of the palm-trees, fringing, with long miles of green, the banks of the glorious old river.

NUBIA, *A Doorway in the Temple of Kalabshe c1857* 1810E (DETAIL)

NUBIA, *The Temple of Kalabshe c1857* 1808

NUBIA, *The Temple of Kalabsha 2004* N209008K

The Temple of Kalabasha (termed Kalabashe by Frith) today is sited just south of the High Dam, about 30 miles north of its original location (shown in photograph 1808, page 81). Its 13,000 blocks of stone were moved in 1962–63. It was begun under the later Ptolemies, and continued under the Romans, but never completed. The temple is dedicated to the Nubian form of Horus (Mandulis), and to Isis and Osiris. Frith's image shows the building buried in rubble, but now the red sandstone structure rises above the waters of the lake on a headland, and it is clearly visible from the Aswan dam. The granite gate of the temple has been moved to the Egyptian Museum in Berlin.

FRITH'S NOTES TO PHOTOGRAPH 1808 *(page 81)*

The Temple of Kalabshe is situated about forty-four miles beyond Assouan. It occupies the site of the ancient Talmis. Our view is taken from the hills which rise abruptly behind it. The spectator is looking towards the south, and obtains as satisfactory a view of the whole plan of an Egyptian temple as could well be desired. Observe the narrow strip of land running to a point in the distance, with a belt of palm-trees (two or three of the elegant Doum palm interspersed) on the water's edge: this is a fair specimen of the habitable territory which constitutes Nubia. The temple-quay extended to the river, and the immense edifice stretched entirely across the valley, and ran some distance by excavation into the rocky hills. The material for its construction was at hand; the whole neighbourhood of the temple being a vast quarry. In the foreground of my picture, to the left of the group of figures, is a wall of this quarry – the accumulation of chippings which covers the whole neighbourhood is wonderful. From the exterior one sees something of the dilapidations of the pylon and walls of circuit; but this view conveys no idea of the extraordinary scene of ruin which the interior presents. The first court is a perfect chaos of immense blocks of stone hurled about in the most fantastic disorder – by what human power one is uterly at a loss to imagine. Again, referring to the picture, it will be seen that the temple-proper is surrounded by two walls of prodigious height and strength, and the whole goves more the idea of a military than of a religious edifice.

ASSOUAN (ASWAN) *c1857* 1830

THE ISLAND OF PHILAE, *The View looking North c1857* 1818

'The Brandy-Sheik roared more hoarsely than ever; he trembled with sham excitement; he grasped a huge stick, and belaboured the men who worked best with relentless idiotcy: he threw himself into the water, swam wildly about, scrambled on board again, and demanded more brandy, or he could not work in the water! For four hours was our wretched boat suffering under the inexpressibly clumsy manoeuvres of these sons of Nature, who thumped her altogether needlessly upon the rocks until she leaked freely.'

For the ancient Egyptians, Aswan was a border town – Nubia lay to the south. Here red granite was quarried; it was used on monuments as far north as Giza. The granite formed a natural barrier in the course of the Nile: the rocks narrowed the river, and outcrops of the hard stone caused rapids. In Frith's time, this stretch of the river was dangerous to negotiate by boat, as he was doing.

Today the town of Aswan is the site of two dams, which regulate the flow of the river: the earlier dam, built between 1898 and 1902 by the British, and the more famous High Dam, built by the Russians. It is the last stopping place for the Nile cruise boats, as they cannot pass beyond the dams on to Lake Nasser. The boats in the foreground of the Frith image have been replaced by cruise boats and graceful feluccas. In early Victorian times, the practice was to rent a dahibieh in Cairo and then to employ a crew. It was sailed rapidly up the Nile with the prevailing northerly wind, and then the visiting of sites was done on the way back up the river as the boat drifted with the current.

Frith's Notes to Photograph 1818 *(opposite)*

The first Cataract of the Nile lies in the direction of the remote distance of our present picture. The granite formation, so conspicuous in the view, commences at Assouan, a town of considerable trade, and of some 800 or 1000 inhabitants, situated immediately at the foot (i.e. north) of the Cataract.

The traveller's boat, in company with a long string of others, being moored at this place, and the Sheik of the Cataract, with his train of assistants, having arrived for the purpose of offering their services – coffee, pipes and compliments having been duly exhausted – the dragoman is desired to hint that we are prepared for business. The shiek coolly remarks, by way of commencement, that our boat is too large to go up the Cataract! We reply that the old-Gentleman knows as well as we do that she has been up twenty times before. 'Taib!' – but he cannot help us up for less than ten pounds – which of course means five – the average sum paid for a boat of medium dimensions. This being arranged, after more coffee and pipes, our visitors take their departure – to return at their option. They have often six or eight engagements upon their hands at once, and we must wait our turn.

On the morning of the ascent, our boat was boarded by some ten or twelve of these Nubian semi-savages, under the nominal command of the most hideous, cracked-voiced, sinister-looking savage of the lot, who soon exhibited another feature of his character – he is a sot, a victim to English brandy, which he drinks neat. An Egyptian in his ordinary state of stupor is sufficiently intolerable; but when he becomes a drunkard, he is indescribably disagreeable. Of course I gave strict orders that no brandy should be given him; but I have reason to think that our dragoman supplied him from his private stock, lest he should resent the affront, and knock us to pieces on the rocks.

Presently his huge bony face glowed with an unmeaning alcoholic energy; his great blood-shot eyes rolled about fiercely; he threw off one scrap of his garments after another; his voice was hollow and husky, and his manner, although savagely determined, was alarmingly confused. But the ship was under his charge, and something must be done – so off we went. Past the island of Elephantine – now utterly despoiled of its once beautiful temple – away amongst masses of smoothly rounded granite, tumbled together in most fantastic shapes; the six miles from Assouan to the series of rapids or falls which constitute the 'First Cataract', is really a charming bit of sailing.

At length we drew up, in company with four or five other boats, at the foot of the chief cataract, where we were boarded by two or three other sheiks, each with his train of dependents, until we had probably thirty or forty on board, and as many more were squatting about on the rocks, to assist in case of need. A rope was attached to the bows of the boat, the other end was carried ashore, and thence commenced a series of plunges, wrigglings, and thumps on the part of our craft, and of bluster, confusion and noise upon that of our savages, which would be perfectly indescribable, but for that concise and convenient phrase, 'that it defies description'. The Brandy-Sheik roared more hoarsely than ever; he trembled with sham excitement; he grasped a huge stick, and belaboured the men who worked best with relentless idiotcy: he threw himself into the water, swam wildly about, scrambled on board again, and demanded more brandy, or he could not work in the water! For four hours was our wretched boat suffering under the inexpressibly clumsy manoeuvres of these sons of Nature, who thumped her altogether needlessly upon the rocks until she leaked freely. For the great haul – where the water descends some three or four feet, in a very narrow channel, at an angle of about 55 degrees – we had probably a hundred hands employed. The fiendish uproar, and the impotent bustle of the scene, would be in the highest degree ludicrous, if it were not so insufferably provoking. A dozen English sailors, with a small windlass, would take the boat up easily in half the time. Yet some travellers speak with raptures of the 'savage faculty' displayed in the ascent!

THE ISLAND OF PHILAE, *The Colonnade c1857* 1826

THE ISLAND OF PHILAE, *On the Approach c1857* 1833E

'Observe, especially, the peculiarly bold and quaint formation of the granite rock, and the singularly harmonious effect of the old Egyptian architecture, rising, like a vision of a giant fairy-land, from the midst of these weird stones and waters; for one becomes accustomed to look upon the old river itself – from its physical peculiarities, and its ruins, and its crocodiles – as being, at any rate, largely implicated in all these mysteries and wonders.'

FACSIMILE REPRODUCTION OF FRANCIS FRITH'S NOTES TO PHOTOGRAPH 1833 (OPPOSITE)

THE APPROACH TO PHILÆ.

HIS is one of the few views which a photograph can render without, perhaps, greatly detracting from its artistic fame. Everybody has sketched it—many clever artists have painted it—Murray has engraved it for his "Guide," and now, in these later days, the Sún himself condescends to pigmify it, and pop it bodily into the box which your artist provided. And it is a view which can bear all this treatment—this freedom of travellers—this robbery—above all, this unflattering mechanical picture-making, without loss of beauty or interest.

We recollect to have exhausted, in a previous article, our philosophy of the combination of causes which give to the Island of Philæ its just fame for impressive loveliness: several of those features may be gathered from a study of this picture. Observe, especially, the peculiarly bold and quaint formation of the granite rock, and the singularly harmonious effect of the old Egyptian architecture, rising, like a vision of a giant fairy-land, from the midst of these weird stones and waters; for one becomes accustomed to look upon the old river itself—from its physical peculiarities, and its ruins, and its crocodiles—as being, at any rate, largely implicated in all these mysteries and wonders. How well do I recollect that it was a moment of happy excitement when our party, after being hauled up the cataract, reached the point from which my view is taken. In all sincerity, we were deeply impressed by the combined beauty and interest of the scene. It has been well, but too often, said that the priests of old Egypt judiciously chose this spot as the seat of their most sacred and mysterious rites. It was well feigned to be the burial-place of Osiris; and the oath, "By him who sleeps in Philæ," was an oath of solemn sounding, and poetic significance. I think I recollect, too, that the place was ingeniously rendered yet more sacred by the necessary resurrection of this deity. His consort, Isis, was also appropriately worshipped here; and, not less consistently followed, in due time, to complete the honour and sanctity of the spot, the birth of their son, the god Horus.

The ridge of granite rocks commencing here, then forming the first cataract, and losing itself six miles below, at Assouan, constitutes the boundary between Egypt and Nubia. Above this spot, the strip of cultivable land on each bank of the river is very small—perhaps not averaging more than a quarter of a mile in width. The inhabitants have been celebrated by many travellers for their beauty of figure and feature, and for the rich bronze colour of their skins. The item of feature I should be strongly inclined to dispute with any traveller not better qualified, by his opportunities, of forming a judgment than I myself have enjoyed. The women, for the most part, are severely hideous; the only interesting feature that I remarked in them is that they wear their black hair—stiff and shiny with a life-long accumulation of castor-oil—in innumerable little black twists, *precisely as we see the hair-dress of women represented in the sculptures of three thousand years ago*—a most striking illustration of the perpetuity of a singular national custom. Some travellers—amongst them Dr. Brugsch—discern also a strong resemblance in the physiognomy of these natives, to that of the ordinary type of feature represented in Egyptian sculpture.

THE ISLAND OF PHILAE *c1857* 1825E

ABOVE RIGHT: THE ISLAND OF AGILKIA, *The Colonnade 1997* A371001K

ABOVE LEFT: THE ISLAND OF PHILAE, *Pharaoh's Bed c1857* 1820 (DETAIL)

BELOW LEFT: THE ISLAND OF AGILKIA, *Trajan's Kiosk 1997* A371002K

The island of Agilkia was reshaped to resemble Philae after the Aswan dam was built – the temple on Philae was then moved there.

There can be little doubt from both the quantity of images Francis Frith took, and the way that he wrote about the site, that out of all the antiquities he saw in Egypt and the Holy Land, Philae made one of the strongest impressions. It had already made its appearance in many engravings by David Roberts, and in a famous painting by Roberts dated 1843. Many other artists were drawn by the beauty of the site. In 1847 Jean-François Portaels painted a view of Trajan's kiosk that echoed the image Roberts had painted and anticipated the images that Francis Frith was to take.

Writers, too, were inspired by the site. In 1827 a Dr Madden listed it among his four greatest sights, and Robert Curzon in 1833 returned there three times, saying that apart from the pyramids, there was no greater sight in Egypt. There can be no wonder, then, at Frith's strong reaction, which echoes the poeticism of previous visitors. His photographs seemed to be based on Roberts's views (1819E, on page 97 and 1820, on page 93, for instance), although some viewpoints are undoubtedly of his own choosing.

The Temple of Philae is in fact a relatively modern one in the context of ancient Egypt. The earliest structure on the island is the Kiosk of Nectanabo I (380–362 BC), although there is evidence of a structure of Taharqa (690–664BC). Most of the buildings visible today and in Frith's time date from the Greek and Roman eras. The dominant main pylon gate dates to the time of Ptolemy XII (80–51BC), although parts of the temple date to the reigns of the earlier Ptolemies. The later parts can be dated to the reigns of the Roman emperors Hadrian and Trajan. The temple owes its fame to being the cult centre of the goddess Isis. This cult travelled throughout the Roman Empire, and had a huge following. So important indeed was it, that it was exempt from the edict of Theodosius in AD 390 ordering the closing of all pagan temples. It thus became the last functioning Egyptian temple, and contains the last hieroglyphic inscription, dated to AD 394. The temple was forcibly closed by the Emperor Justinian in the mid 6th century. It then became a church of the Bishop Theodore.

In recent times it was flooded by the building of the first Aswan dam, and when the building of the second dam threatened to destroy it completely, it was surrounded by a coffer dam, dismantled and rebuilt on the island of Agilkia – the island was reshaped to resemble Philae. These works were not completed until 1980 (see A371002k on page 91).

The photograph of the kiosk of Trajan on the island of Philae (1820, opposite) was justly famous in its own time. The British Journal of Photography of March 1860 calls it 'a most effective picture' and 'little, if anything, short of perfection'. Today this view has been lost to history: the island of Philae has been submerged under the waters created in the gap between the low dam at Aswan and the new High Dam. The level of the water we see here indicates that Frith was in Aswan at a time when the Nile was not in flood, during the winter months. Although the resemblance between the old image and the new is remarkable, the large retaining wall visible below the kiosk is much reduced in size, since the island is completely new.

THE ISLAND OF PHILAE, *Pharaoh's Bed c1857* 1820

Francis Frith's Notes to Photograph 1820 *(page 93)*

Philae is the most beautiful thing in Egypt; and the temple, absurdly called Pharoah's Bed, is the most beautiful thing upon the island. I flatter myself, too, somewhat, upon the quality of my Photograph, – light transparent shadows, sweet half-tones, oh discriminating Public! It is true that the temple outdoes the Tower of Babel, not only 'reaching unto the heavens', but robbing the picture of well-nigh all its sky – that feature so essential to the picturesque in landscape. But what could I do? I must give that scrap of water, and the Nile boat (a favourite anchorage for travellers' dahibiehs, this nook), and I could not falsify the height of the bank, as I see most artists have done, to suit the proportions of my picture.

I have a great mind to write some verses; certes, if I contemplated an epic, I should establish myself upon the Island of Philae to write it. It is just one of those places which one is sure that the shades of Muses must haunt – so beautiful, so still (there are now no inhabitants upon the island), so dreamy, yet so richly suggestive. The fact is, that very little that is appropriate to the special subject of my picture can be said in plain prose, – unless, indeed, I had a genius for architectural detail, and a frantic love of feet and inches; which I rejoice, for thy sake, dear Public, I have not. Yet, let me see; the building is hypaethral – that is, its building did not contemplate a roof. What a charming compliment is this to the fair, cloudless, maiden sky, which always smiles over this delicious clime! It was built by a Ptolemy, or a Caesar, so that it is only about two thousand years old! No wonder that it looks so fresh! – and yet, oh wrong-headed early-dynasty man, would not even twenty hundred years in any other climate under heaven have accumulated some soil and stains – investing the pile with the sombre grey and green livery of antiquity, and gnawing the soft smooth sandstone into a condition resembling that of an old ripe Stilton cheese? But here, on the confines of Nubia, where there is no smoke, no damp, not even dew, the glorious and unique temple looks literally as clean and fresh as it did the year it was completed. There is no sculpture upon it. Beneath the temple may be seen the remains of a river-wall and quay, which extended nearly round the island.

The dahibieh here represented, being on her downward voyage, is despoiled of her greatest ornament – the towering and picturesque lateen sail, the long 'yard' of which is now lashed over the whole length of the ship. This boat cost our party thirty pounds per month, including the wages of the Rais and ten men, who 'find themselves'. The pioneers of what is now the 'Nile excursion', were accustomed to sink their boats for a few days, in order to rid them of unwelcome tenants; but the dahibiehs now-a-days are smart and cleanly – often luxorious, some few having, besides excellent canteens, &c., very fair libraries of European books, and even pianofortes!

THE ISLAND OF PHILAE, *A Group of Palms c1857* 1824E

This image is once again of Trajan's kiosk. The roof, perhaps of wooden beams, is missing, or the building was never completed. Each of the capitals of the columns has a slightly different design, and their composite nature marks them out as belonging to the Greek or Roman period. The kiosk was once the formal entrance to the temple complex. This view and Number 1820 (page 93) were two of the most commonly pictured Philae scenes in Victorian times.

FRANCIS FRITH'S NOTES TO PHOTOGRAPH 1824E

There are two objects – frequent accompaniments of Egyptian scenery – which few artists have succeeded in representing truthfully, viz., the camel and the palm-tree. With respect to the former, he must be a bold, as well as a skilful man, who dares trust to paper, forms which would surely be hideously ugly, had not the miraculous hand of Nature blended them with such wonderful adaptation and consistency as invests the creature with a sort of quaint beauty, which, in the hands of Wilson and Goodall,is exceedingly picturesque. Artists of inferior talent do not dare to draw a camel ugly enough. Your animal's nose, sir, is not "Roman" enough by half, and he carries it far too high. Moreover, if he belongs to that old Bedawee, his condition is also too high. You may cut him very nearly in two, with the inner line of his hind-leg. That posterior waist of his should be almost as slender as a wasp's. Then you have

'They must be drawn with pre-Raphaelite care – every leafstalk must be pricked thoughtfully into the stem as though you were budding a rose; and each one must droop – oh how daintily! and with what sweet regard to the attitudes of her neighbours all around.'

pinched his feet unmercifully – he is not intended to show off in Regent Street in a pair of Paris boots – on the contrary, he requires a series of pads, about the shape and size of railway-buffers to 'flop' down on the top of a square foot of sand. Work at him! – you will be a good draughtsman by the time you have made him as ugly as a camel, and as handsome!

The case of the palm is analagous to that of the camel, although rather the reverse of it. You, miss, are afraid of beauty – you are passionately fond it it, I know – you would give anything to be yourself as graceful as a palm-tree! Do you ever twist yourself into a sort of Hogarth's line of beauty and grace when you want to be effective and 'not stiff?' I hope not. Then why did you draw that palm tree so? – why did you not rather produce the bole with the aid of a parallel ruler? Look at the tall palm-tree in my picture, 50 or 60 feet high, and as straight as an arrow. So far it is easy enough; but it will require more skill and careful study to do justice to its crown of leaves. It is the very perfection of symmetrical disorder – one of the finest examples in nature of picturesque formality – every leaf, every leaflet is alike, yet dissimilar – all bend gracefully from the axis to the point, but no two in the same curve. They must be drawn with pre-Raphaelite care – every leafstalk must be pricked thoughtfully into the stem as though you were budding a rose; and each one must droop – oh how daintily! and with what sweet regard to the attitudes of her neighbours all around. Thou couldst not set thyself, O lady, a more congenial task …

The building seen through the trees is the hypethral temple, called Pharoah's Bed, of which we have already given a nearer view. The sides exhibit five columns, and the ends four: the inter-columnar wall being nearly half the height of the columns. Dr. Richardson suggests that it was probably exhibited in ancient times as the tomb of Osiris, who was supposed to be buried here. 'By him who sleeps in Philae', was the most sacred oath of the Thebiad.

Photograph 1819E (opposite), both in its title and its composition, is the closest to a Roberts's print. He too drew the site from the south, and the framing of his image is virtually identical. Roberts did exercise some artistic licence: the clutter of granite outcrops that mark the first cataract which we can see in Frith's image are largely absent in the Roberts engraving.

THE ISLAND OF PHILAE, *The South End c1857* 1819E

THE ISLAND OF BIGGEH, *The View looking South c1857* 1816E

VIEW FROM THE ISLAND OF BIGGEH, LOOKING SOUTH.

IT would be difficult to find a scene which might illustrate better than this, both the character of the scenery around Philæ (especially on the adjoining Island of Biggeh), and the aspect of the river's course through Nubia; for we have now entered that country. But we will first speak of the extraordinary granite formation which is here displayed with so much character. The whole island seems to be a gigantic pile of detached blocks of granite of every conceivable shape and size, tumbled together in the most picturesque confusion. Some of the pieces exhibit rough fractured surfaces, but the greater part are rounded and worn glassy-smooth by the action of the elements; and in places where they are reached by the Nile floods, are absolutely coated with a vitrified surface, which at once suggests the agency of fire. This granite formation first appears (as has been before stated) at Assouan, some six or seven miles north, and continues with some interruptions through the whole of the cataract-district, which will be more particularly described when I come to speak of my journey in Ethiopia. Sir G. Wilkinson says—"On the rocks here, as on the road from Assouan to Philæ, are numerous inscriptions of the early times of the Pharaohs of the 16th, 17th, 18th, and 19th dynasties, several of which mention the holy object of their writers, who came to adore the gods of the district, while others merely present the names of the monarchs themselves. Some relate to the granite blocks cut and removed in their reigns, and others to the victories gained by them over the Ethiopians, the people of Cush." And of the remarkable pinnacle of rock on the right of the picture, the same writer says—"There is also a rock opposite the north end of Philæ, remarkable for its elevated appearance and general form; but there is no reason to suppose that any religious idea was attached to it, as some have imagined, and much less that it was *Abaton*," a term used by ancient writers, sometimes apparently with reference to this island, and sometimes to Philæ.

The district of Nubia, which we are now entering, extends from Philæ to Wady Halfa, a distance of about 220 miles. It presents for the most part just such a landscape as the one on the opposite side of the river in this view, viz., a very narrow strip of cultivated land, often merely the sloping bank of the stream where the inundation has deposited patches of its fertile mud amongst the rocks—indeed, in many places the rocks descend sheer down into the river—with here and there a palm-grove and a village, backed by a range of hot and barren hills, beyond which on either side stretches a boundless desert. Yet this district, which now looks so inhospitable, must at some period have maintained a considerable population, for we find in it no less than twelve or fourteen temple ruins, some of them of great magnitude and interest.

I believe that the earliest known Egyptian conqueror of the country is Thothmes the First. There is a monument in the Island of Argo in Ethiopia, known as the "Golden Stone," which bears his name. This was about 1500 years B.C. The Second and Third Thothmes appear to have extended their conquests still further. The Romans under Petronius, prefect of Egypt in the time of Augustus, also penetrated as far as Napata, the ancient capital of Ethiopia; but it does not appear that the intermediate monarchs maintained their supremacy in Ethiopia, and perhaps not even in Nubia, although it is probable that the Ptolemies regained possession of the latter district. In Strabo's time the Island of Philæ belonged in common to the Egyptians and Ethiopians. In modern days Nubia was virtually independent of the Egyptian rule, until Mahommed Ali, pursuing the fugitive Mamalukes who retreated thither, thoroughly subjected the country. The inhabitants were disarmed, and have ever since been quiet tax-paying serfs of the ruling pasha of Egypt.

'The whole island seems to be a gigantic pile of detached blocks of granite of every conceivable shape and size, tumbled together in the most picturesque confusion.'

FACSIMILE REPRODUCTION OF FRANCIS FRITH'S NOTES TO PHOTOGRAPH 1816E

The island of Biga (as it is now transcribed) was once more important than the more famous Philae which lay opposite it. It was held by the ancient Egyptians in the Graeco-Roman period to be both the grave of Osiris and also the source of the Nile itself. A sanctuary had been built there in ancient times, and by the time of the Greeks the location had become so sacred that no one was allowed on the island, giving it its Greek name of Abaton, meaning 'forbidden place'.

With the fall of paganism, the temple was converted to a Christian church, and it is this arch that is to be seen in 1831E.

The island provided David Roberts with more of his views, and thus Francis Frith was once again following in his footsteps. However, Frith's photograph Number 1831E does seem to show that Roberts's engraving had taken some liberties with reality, as the position of Philae through the arch is in fact completely different. Roberts seems to have made the island rather more prominent.

The image of Biga looking south (1816E, page 98) seems to show Frith's developing tent erected in the shade behind a boulder in the centre left of the picture. The shadow is as black as his tent was, and to keep in the shade behind a boulder out of the direct heat of the sun would make sense with such volatile chemicals.

The 'antiquities' of the title in photograph 1832 on page 101 are probably the remains of medieval tombs, which were erected here as part of the church complex.

THE ISLAND OF BIGGEH, *A Roman Arch c1857* 1831E

THE ISLAND OF BIGGEH, *Antiquities c1857* 1832E

FRITH'S NOTES TO PHOTOGRAPH 1832E *(previous page)*

The interest of the Island of Biggeh to the traveller is threefold: 1st, its peculiarly striking and bold granite formation, the large detached blocks being piled upon one another in the most fantastic style, and rising in some places to pinnacles of considerable height; 2nd, its antiquities, which consist of the ruins of a temple and sundry scattered pieces of statuary &c.; and lastly, the splendid views which it commands of the neighbouring Island of Philae. Most travellers climb to the edge of the rocks overhanging the village (vide Photograph); and I imagine that few are willing soon to relinquish the view which is obtained from thence. The Island of Philae, with its temple ruins and its scattered palm trees, lies like a map below, and all around it flows the noble river, its banks beautifully diversified with rock and sandy nook, patches of bright green cornland, and groves of dark graceful palms. It will be observed that a small Arab village clusters around the two antique columns in the centre of the picture. The boys and girls, too, from this village are frequently seen astride pieces of palm-trees, navigating across to the other island in search of wood, &c., for fuel. As for your artist, his clearest recollections are of a luxurious and effective field-day hereaway, for he rigged up his photographic tent in the small boat, and was pulled about by his shiny black Nubians from dawn till dusk, just landing and knocking off a view wherever and whenever the fancy struck him. Ah, brother Photographers! with a sky like that, and such subjects, and a bottle of splendid pale – not ale – but, collodion, you can only imagine the glory of such a day.

In the centre of my view are the ruins of a temple, which Sir G. Wilkinson says was dedicated to Athor, apparently commenced by Euergetes I (B.C. 246), and completed by Ptolemy the Elder, son of Auletes, by Augustus, and by others of the Caesars; but, from the presence of a red granite statue behind it, there is reason to believe that an older edifice had previously existed here, of the time of a Pharoah, either Thothmes III or Amunoph II. Amongst the mounds is a stela of red granite, bearing the name of Amasis. The arch, inserted at a late period in the centre of the building, is of Christian origin; and it is evident that the early Christians occupied the temples both of this island and of Philae, converting them into churches, and plastering over the offensive emblems of idolatrous worship with mud. The hieroglyphic name of Biggeh appears to be 'Senmaut'. Upon many of the prominent granite rocks, both in the island and on the opposite bank of the river, are found hieroglyphic inscriptions of the times of the early Pharoahs; some of them record that their writers visited these sacred places to pay their devotions to the presiding deities, or that in their reigns certain immense granite blocks had been quarried and removed ...

'Ah, brother Photographers! with a sky like that, and such subjects, and a bottle of splendid pale – not ale – but, collodion, you can only imagine the glory of such a day.'

PHILAE, *A Doum Palm and a Ruined Mosque c1857* 1815E

Photograph 1815E (previous page) was entitled 'Doum Palm and Ruined Mosque near Philae'. The site is now almost certainly under water.
Although Frith does not say so, this building is most likely to be the tomb of Qubbet el-Hawwa, a local saint, which lies to the west back at Aswan opposite the town.
The doum palm, with its forked trunks and spiky leaves, is a distinctive tree. Its nuts are often found in burials. An example is the burial of two workmen at the workers' village at Deir el-Medina. Sennefer's tomb contained three plates of fruit including doum nuts, and more were found in the tomb of Satre. Frith explicitly states that the nuts are inedible, and that they are used as a form of 'vegetable ivory'; this might make us think that the nuts were provided for the dead because of their longevity.
However, it may be that Frith is mistaken, especially as there are pictures of doum palms in fruit being harvested by the ancient Egyptians on several papyri. In his 'Life of the Ancient Egyptians', Eugen Strouhal describes doum palm fruit either being eaten raw, soaked in water, or made into a sweet pulp.
In his accompanying text to this picture, Frith gives us a very vivid impression of how he worked, and also a rather touching image of his mother cleaning his shirts!

Francis Frith's Notes to Photograph 1815E

'It may interest my brethren of the Black Art (as my mother calls it when she overhauls my shirts as they come from the wash) to know something about my photographic apparatus and modus operandi. Know, then, that for the purpose of making large pictures (20 inches by 16), I had constructed in London a wicker-work carriage on wheels, which was, in fact, both camera and developing room, and occasionally sleeping room; so that the doctor whom I heard at a meeting of the Photographic Society a year or two ago ridiculing the rage for large pictures, and proposing, as the ultima thule of extravagance which his playful fancy could suggest, "that men should have their cameras upon wheels, and large enough to sleep in," (a remark which raised a hearty laugh through the room), committed an error common with wits - his remark was much less facetious and imaginative than he supposed. This carriage of mine, then, being entirely overspread with a loose cover of white sailcloth to protect it from the sun, was a most conspicuous and mysterious-looking vehicle, and excited amongst the Egyptian populace a vast amount of ingenious speculation as to its uses. The idea, however, which seemed the most reasonable, and therefore obtained the most, was that therein, with right laudable and jealous care, I transported from place to place - my - harem! It was full of moon-faced beauties, my wives all! - and great was the respect and consideration which this view of the case procured for me!

The quarry in photograph 1844E (below) lies in the south of Egypt, about 50 miles north of Aswan. It is described by Amelia Edwards in 'One Thousand Miles up the Nile' in 1877, and it was painted by David Roberts in 1838 and by Bridgeman in 1874.
The quarries date to the New Kingdom period, although there are images on the rocks that date as far back as the pre-dynastic period. The quarries lie mostly on the east bank of the Nile, but there is a rock-cut temple of King Horemheb (1323–1295BC) on the west bank, together with other New Kingdom shrines. The Frith image shows the angular cutting of the sandstone; this was no mean achievement with only copper and stone tools.

HAGAR SILSILIS, *A View in the Quarries c1857* 1844E

FRANCIS FRITH'S NOTES TO PHOTOGRAPH 1844E

After about twenty miles more of somewhat monotonous sailing, we reach a remarkable spot in the river - where its channel is considerably narrowed, and where a singular column of rock, which has been left in quarrying ...

The principal quarries (which I will first describe) are situated on the eastern bank of the river, where also stood the ancient town of Silsilis, of which nothing remains. The grottoes, which contain many interesting sculptures and paintings, are on the western side. There is every reason to suppose that most of the great buildings of Egypt, especially of Thebes and Philae, were built of sandstone supplied by these quarries: and, I must needs echo the remark which has been made by every one who has seen or described them, that if the monuments themselves had all perished, the quarries of Hager Silsilis would be sufficient to establish the monumental fame of ancient Egypt. The manner in which the stone has been cut may be observed as distinctly as though one saw the men at work. Every chisel mark is there, sharp and clean; the wedge-holes seem as though they had just fallen asunder, or were but yesterday prepared for the wooden plugs. The work was well and cleanly done. There was no unnecessary waste of good material; but here and there an isolated wall of faulty stone stands boldly out across the quarry. The excavations extend for more than a mile north and south, and penetrate into the mountains to a considerable distance.

'The view from this point is most extraordinary ... It reminds you of some grand old giant, buried to the shoulders – not dead yet, but overpowered and imprisoned by some potent spell – majestic in his helplessness.'

Francis Frith's Notes to Photograph 1835 *(opposite)*

As the traveller's dahibieh glides noiselessly to the south, on the bosom of the father of rivers, the low green banks, with their mud villages and palm tree groves, are occasionally relieved by a bold projection of rock standing out into the stream. On such an eminence, nearly five hundred miles south of Cairo, and one hundred miles beyond Thebes, we welcome the ruins of Koum Ombos. Here the river makes a wide majestic bend, and on the sandbanks opposite the temple may often be seen, basking in the hot noon-day sun, two or three fine crocodiles. Mooring to the shore, as the light breeze entirely fails us, we scramble up to the temple area. But ere we begin the ascent, we pause to consider the dimensions of the gigantic blocks of granite and sandstone, covered with that strange handwriting of the infancy of time. We feel that they ought to be measured, but it constantly occurs to us that fifty people have done this before us; and so, passing the dilapidated pylon, we stand in a few minutes on the spot from which my view is taken. The view from this point is most extraordinary: the accumulated sands of ages have buried this once magnificent pile to the capitals of the columns, and its stunted height strikes you as strangely disproportionate to the vastness of its other dimensions, and the immense size of the stones. It reminds you of some grand old giant, buried

LEFT: KOUM OMBOS, *From the North East c1857* 1836

KOUM OMBOS, *Near View c1857* 1835

'It is aggravating to know that a money-grubbing, sugar-baking pasha (Abbas) has had split up and carried off many of these superb blocks, to be used in the building of his sugar refineries, of which brand of trade, and many others, the pasha usurps a monopoly.'

to the shoulders – not dead yet, but overpowered and imprisoned by some potent spell – majestic in his helplessness. Gazing on the magnificence of the visible portion of this splendid ruin, it does not seem too much to hope that Koum Ombos may at some period be released from this sandy sepulchre, and the men of three thousand years hence may look on his wonderful proportions, and admire the prowess of the men of three thousand years ago. Turn to the picture, and compare the size of the sculptured blocks of stone with the two Nile sailors standing near one of them, for of such blocks is the whole temple built. It is aggravating to know that a money-grubbing, sugar-baking pasha (Abbas) has had split up and carried off many of these superb blocks, to be used in the building of his sugar refineries, of which brand of trade, and many others, the pasha usurps a monopoly.

The only remains of antiquity which seem to have suggested an idea to the modern architects of Egypt are the crude brick walls which appear to have enclosed the sacred precincts of many of the temples. At Koum Ombos some prodigious masses of this kind of wall remain. Think of the climate in which even unbaked Nile-mud bricks will stand square and solid for two thousand years! Sir G. Wilkinson says of this temple: – 'It was founded in the reign of Ptolemy Philometer, continued by his brother Physcon (who is introduced, as usual, with his queens, the two Cleopatras), and finished by Auletes or Neus Dionysus'. Thus, although the principal ruins date from only shortly before the Christian era, there are traces of much earlier structures, some probably of the early epoch of the Pharoahs of the eighteenth dynasty. In the steep bank facing the river are remains of an approach, beautifully sculptured ...

We are now sixteen miles above the Rock of the Chain, and twenty-four short of Assouan, the boundary of Upper Egypt. The view (1836) is taken from the north-east corner of the temple enclosure, where the sand, which has half-buried the temple, is drifted within the crude brick wall of circuit level with its top; and hence we have a fine prospect, not only of the ruin, but of a large extent of the Nile Valley. The temple is situated on a promontory on the eastern bank of the river, which here makes a bend to the west-ward. Its course through the landscape is indicated to some extent by the groves of palm-trees which are for the most part only found upon its banks. The intervening country is cultivated chiefly by hand-irrigation, and produces crops of grain, castor-oil, and cotton: the latter seems to be the staple crop. In th extreme distance is the dim outline of the hills of the western desert.

Standing close to the Nile on a rise in the bank which marks a bend in the river, Kom Ombo (Frith's Koum Ombos) is a much visited ruin by the modern cruise ships. It lies to the south of Edfu between it and Aswan. It is a unique temple in Egypt in that it has two sanctuaries, one dedicated to the crocodile god Sobek, and the other to a form of the hawk god Horus. It was begun by Ptolemy VI (180–145BC) and completed by Ptolemy XII (80–51BC).

This was a favoured spot for Victorian travellers, doubtless because of its scenic position close to the Nile, and Roberts made many paintings as well as engravings of this temple. Its ruined state lends an air of romance to the site which still remains, despite the fact that the site has been cleared and partially reconstructed. At dusk the reliefs are particularly impressive.

KOUM OMBOS (KOM OMBO), *Bound Captives 1997* K170001K

EDFOU, *The Great Pylon c1857* 1841

The temple of Edfu is the most complete temple in Egypt. It is dedicated to the god Horus, and stands on the site of an earlier New Kingdom construction. The present building was begun in 237 BC by Ptolemy III (246–221BC) and completed in 57 BC by Ptolemy XII. Thanks to the well-preserved inscriptions here, we have a good knowledge of its construction history, and of the daily ritual in the temple.

Frith's picture is taken from much the same point as David Roberts's engraving of November 1838. It shows the way that the sand and debris had built up around the structure, and in front of the giant gateway we can see the remains of huts from the town. These have now been cleared, although the temple still stands in the centre of the town of Edfu, some distance from the Nile. It is one of the most impressive monuments in Egypt.

ERMENT, *Cleopatra's Temple 1857* 1848E

THEBES, *Medinet Habu, The View in the First Court c1857* 1866E

THEBES, *The Temple Palace at Medinet Habu c1857* 1865E

THE TEMPLE PALACE, MEDINET-HABOO.

O those who have followed us through our series of illustrations of ancient Egyptian architecture, the ruin here given will at once appear altogether strange and dissimilar. It is indeed unique. It was the palace of Rameses III., and is the only building of this character which has outlasted the ages of demolition and decay, to which the structures of the Nile Valley have been subjected, and nothing but proportions so prodigiously massive as to be almost immovable by human agency, has saved those that remain. This palace is, therefore, a most interesting object to the antiquarian. It is situated to the south of the Temple-Propylæ, which were erected by the same monarch, and closely contiguous to them. The square windows alone would be sufficient to distinguish it from all the other existing antiquities of Egypt. The style of its hieroglyphic embellishment is also peculiar—representing, in the interior of the chambers, various scenes of domestic life. To begin with the exterior—upon one of the wings of the building appears the king, of gigantic stature, slaughtering his enemies in battle; his divine protector, Amun Ra, extends to him the sword of victory, &c. The conquered tribes are next led into captivity, headed by their respective kings, whose countenances are very characteristic. In one of the halls is the celebrated chess-playing scene, in which the king is surrounded by his *hareem*, one of whom he tenderly caresses, and with others he is engaged in a game which is not actually that of chess, but bears a greater resemblance to draughts. Some of his attendant ladies present him with flowers, or are engaged in fanning him; but they are all obliged to stand in his presence, the king alone being seated on an elegant divan. Sir G. Wilkinson says that the queen is not among them; and that her cartouche-oval is always blank, where it occurs, throughout the building. The game here represented is also seen in the grottoes of Beni Hassan, where it dates as far back as 1700 years before the Christian era, in the time of Osirtasin—the contemporary of Joseph. In another part of the building occur ornamented balustrades, each supported by four figures of African and northern barbarians, and the summit of the whole pavilion was crowned with a row of shields—the battlements of Egyptian architecture.

The original design of the palace was probably much more extensive than these ruins at first sight indicate. In front was a paved raised platform, and in connection with the wings were many other chambers which are now totally destroyed.

'In one of the halls is the celebrated chess-playing scene, in which the king is surrounded by his harem, one of whom he tenderly caresses, and with others he is engaged in a game which is not actually that of chess, but bears a greater resemblance to draughts.'

FACSIMILE REPRODUCTION OF FRANCIS FRITH'S NOTES TO PHOTOGRAPH 1865E (PREVIOUS PAGE)

THEBES, *The Pylon Gateway at Medinet Habu c1857* 1867

THEBES, *The Osiridae Pillar at Medinet Habu c1857* 1867E

THEBES, *New Excavations at Medinet Habu c1860* 1868E

Medinet Habu is the mortuary temple of Rameses III (1184–1153BC), and it is the best preserved of all the mortuary temples on the west bank. The site, known as Djamet, was sacred long before the time of Rameses III, for it was the supposed burial place of the nine gods. It was also sacred long after the temple fell into disrepair, as it became a Christian community called Djeme, centred on a church built in the second courtyard (this seems to have been misnamed by Frith 'the first court'). Pillars of this church can be seen in photograph 1866E (page 111).

One of the earliest temples on the site was begun by Hatshepsut (1473–1458BC) and Tuthmosis III (1479–1425BC). It stands to the right of the main entrance. The main gate Frith rightly describes as unusual: 'Its peculiar large square windows are novelties in Egyptian architecture.' This gateway was in fact modelled on a Western Asiatic migdol, or fortress.

The rooms in this gateway seem to have acted as a harem; their walls are covered with representations of the king surrounded by the royal women playing senet, a kind of board game. This gate is clearly seen in photograph 1865E (page 112).

That the caption to 1865E is 'the Temple Palace' is accurate; today it is possible to stand in the throne room of the king in front of the dais on which the throne was located. It is also possible to stand in the king's shower, which is just behind the throne room – this was almost certainly the location of the conspiracy that ended his life.

The Osiridae pillar (1867E, page 114) is still there and little changed, but the excavations over the years have cleared and tidied the site. The pillar represents the king in the form of Osiris, with his arms crossed on his chest. This representation is appropriate to a temple whose purpose was the commemoration of the dead king and the continuance of his cult.

Photograph 1868E (page 115) is titled 'New Excavations'. This highly interesting view dates from later than the other images of Medinet Habu, and was published in the second collection of photographs (1860–61). This means that the image was almost certainly taken on Frith's third visit to Egypt, and thus records the results of Mariette's excavations of 1859, instigated by Said Pasha. The photograph is taken from the rear, northern end of the temple, and looks out over the hypostyle hall towards the pylon gates at the threshold of the first and second courts.

FAR LEFT: THEBES, *Osiridae Statue of Rameses III, Medinet Habu* 2004 T323006K

LEFT: THEBES, *Painted Columns, Medinet Habu 1999* T323001K

RIGHT: *Forms of Osiris*

TOP LEFT: THEBES, *Medinet Habu 2004* T323005K
BOTTOM LEFT: THEBES, *Medinet Habu, the Entrance 2004* T323003K
ABOVE: THEBES, *A Gate in Medinet Habu 2004* T323007K

THEBES, *The Osiridae Pillars and the Great Fallen Colossus c1857* 1850E

Frith was undoubtedly influenced by Roberts in photograph 1850E (previous page). In Roberts's picture the head and shoulders of Rameses II lie bathed in the golden light of sunset, with locals sitting at the statue's base. In Frith's photograph he too has added local colour – two figures sit on the fallen statue. This image of one of the greatest rulers of Egypt fallen into decay was not lost on Shelley, who based his poem 'Ozymandias' on these monuments. The twin of this bust can be seen in the British Museum; it was taken there by Belzoni in 1816.

LEFT: *The Divine Triad of Amun, Mut and Khonsu (father, mother and son)*

THEBES, *The Rameseum from the Air 2004* T323011K

The Rameseum (1852E, opposite) is the funerary temple of Rameses II. It was a large structure, designed to perpetuate his memory and also to provide offerings for his cult, hence the many arched mud-brick store rooms around it. As we can see from the aerial shot, time has not been kind to this monument; like Rameses's tomb in the Valley of the Kings, it is in a poor state of repair.

THEBES, *The Rameseum c1857* 1852E

These great seated statues, which still stand somewhat incongruously amidst the cultivation of the west bank at Thebes, are the last clearly visible remains of what was the huge funeral temple of Amenhotep III, perhaps the greatest king of the 18th dynasty. The statues stood in front of the first pylon gate of the temple; originally they were taller, each with a tall crown on top of the head. They are made of a reddish quartzite, a stone linked to the sun. In front of the right leg of the king, clearly visible in Frith's picture, is a small image of Amenhotep's queen, Tiye. We can see camels, too, which also appear in contemporary paintings of the monument.

An extract from the text accompanying another Frith photograph of the statues gives us a flavour of Victorian tourism, and indeed scenes like this are very familiar to those who go to Egypt today: 'I have reason to know what I am about to write is literally correct, for I had to suspend my operations whilst the party was moving about the bases of the statues, and had nothing to do at the moment but watch anxiously for signs of their departure. But how true soever my story, it will scarcely be believed, that at least two or three of the party spent their whole time on the spot in haggling with the Arabs over paltry purchases, and the moment they were concluded – my word for it – they threw themselves upon their donkeys and rode off to the next "sight", without having raised their eyes to the glorious old statues of Memnon.'

THEBES, *The Statues of Memnon c1857* 1857 (WITH DETAIL BELOW)

THEBES, *The Portico of the Temple of Goorneh c1857* 1851

'This temple is, exteriorly, one of the least imposing of the ruins of Thebes. It is situated not very far from the river, amidst a grove of Tamarisk trees, and its principal feature is the portico, with a single row of pillars, respresented in the view.'

from **FRANCIS FRITH'S NOTES TO PHOTOGRAPH 1851**

Also on the west bank, but at the opposite end of the long series of mortuary temples, lies the temple of Seti I (1294–1279) at Dra Abu el-Naga. Sometimes called Temple Goorneh, it was completed during the co-regency with his son Rameses II, and was in part dedicated to his father Rameses I (1295–1294). Much of the temple does not survive, but what we can see shows the same artistic quality as the temple at Abydos, whose raised reliefs are justly famous. It was the first destination of the sacred boat of Amun on the west bank at Thebes during the important Beautiful Festival of the Valley. In this photograph we see two good examples of the papyrus bundle columns that were popular in the early to mid New Kingdom; other examples are to be found in the temple at Luxor.

VALLEY OF THE TOMBS OF THE KINGS, THEBES.

THERE is nothing in the whole Valley of the Nile which is more grandly characteristic of Old Egypt, or which leaves upon the mind of the traveller a more powerful and lasting impression, than a visit to the Tombs of the Kings, at Thebes. They are situated at a distance of five or six miles from the river, at the extremity of a deep and romantic gorge in the mountains. The entire course of this ravine presents a spectacle of desolate grandeur, which is in the highest degree impressive, and prepares the mind fully to appreciate the effect of the kingly sepulchres to which it leads. There is not a blade of grass, nor a sign of life except when a solitary vulture wheels overhead, or a jackal is seen stealing amongst the hot loose stones. An artificial road has been cut in the bottom of the gorge—this is represented in my view, which is taken from a spot near the termination of the valley, where the tombs commence. Some twenty-seven of these have been discovered, but the entrances are so small as not to be recognisable in a distant general view. At about this place the valley divides into two branches: in the western of which only two tombs have been opened—viz., those of Amenotoph III. and King Ai—both of the eighteenth dynasty; in the eastern branch are found numerous tombs of the kings of the ninteenth and twentieth dynasties; the most celebrated and beautiful of which is that of Seti I., which is named after its modern discoverer, Belzoni. The rock into which these excavations are made, is of the most beautifully compact limestone; the passages and chambers are covered with hieroglyphic sculpture, much of which is still brilliantly coloured.

Professor Brugsch supplies me with the following description of these celebrated tombs:—The Theban tombs are for the most part entered by a passage, leading from a sort of outer court, and often decorated with paintings and inscriptions, into an inner and larger court, corresponding to the pronaos of the temples. From another, and still interior apartment, we descend by a deep, and often perpendicular opening, into the sepulchral chamber, which is usually of a square form. In many cases several descending openings were made in addition to the one leading only to the real place of entombment. The inscriptions and paintings were arranged according to a prescribed order; thus, near the entrance, were the names and titles of the deceased, and a prayer to the rising and setting sun. In the inner chamber were inscribed the praises of the deities presiding over tombs, and in other parts of the sepulchre were various biographical and historic records connected with the life and times of the deceased. So extensive were these places of interment, that the area of the ground-plan of a single private tomb, near Thebes, is 23,809 square feet, and the royal tombs are constructed on a much larger scale.

THEBES, *The Valley of the Tombs of Kings c1857* 1855

'The entire course of this ravine presents a spectacle of desolate grandeur ... There is not a blade of grass, nor a sign of life except when a solitary vulture wheels overhead, or a jackal is seen stealing amongst the hot stones.'

FACSIMILE REPRODUCTION OF FRANCIS FRITH'S NOTES TO PHOTOGRAPH 1855 (OPPOSITE)

The Valley of the Kings (photograph 1855, page 124) must rank as one of the most famous archaeological sites in the world. Thanks to the discovery of the tomb of Tutankhamun (1336–1327BC) in 1922, the valley is familiar to almost anyone with even a minimal interest in the subject. Of course, when Frith took his picture the discovery of the tomb of the boy king lay seventy years in the future, and the easy access that the modern tourist enjoys was still further in the future. However, thanks to the discovery of the tomb of Seti I by Belzoni, the valley was enjoying its first real period of fame; an exhibition about it attracted large crowds in London. The tomb is one of the most beautiful in the valley, which itself contains the tombs of 23 New Kingdom kings. The first king to be buried here was Tuthmosis I (1504–1492BC) in 1492 BC, and the valley remained in use until the burial of Rameses XI (1099–1069BC) in 1070 BC. The remoteness of the place seems to be highlighted by Frith's image. The figures at the base of the cliffs are dwarfed by the pyramidal peak of el-Qurn, which was linked to the snake goddess Meretseger, 'she who loves silence'.

RIGHT: THEBES, KARNAK, *The Hall of Columns 2004* T323008K

OPPOSITE: THEBES, *A Gate 2004* T323010K

Francis Frith paid several visits to this magnificent temple complex. The first was on his initial visit to Egypt in 1857, and the commentary to his photographs was written by himself. He also visited the complex in 1859 in his second and more extensive visit to the Middle East.

It was not until the mid 18th century that Thebes had any recognition as an important location of antiquities; but Napoleon's expedition, and the paintings and etchings of the early years of the 19th century by such artists as David Roberts and Jacob Jacobs, brought the ruins to the attention of a wider public.

Karnak is the single largest religious site ever built by man. It is a collection of temples and sacred areas bounded by an enclosure wall, and it covers an area of 247 acres. The constant rebuilding of the temples on the site makes the exact foundation date difficult to determine. The photographs by Francis Frith that we see here show buildings dating from the New Kingdom and the Late Period. That the site had holy associations long before this is without doubt; indeed, one of the most beautiful buildings to be seen today is the chapel of the Middle Kingdom pharaoh Senwosret I in the Open Air Museum.

The temple complex is primarily devoted to the worship of the god Amun, known later as Amun-Re. He began to gain prominence in the Middle Kingdom when the ruling house came from this area, but it was not until the New Kingdom that Karnak began to become pre-eminent among the religious sites of ancient Egypt.

Today the visitor is amazed by the scale of the Hypostyle Hall. It covers a huge area, far larger than St Peter's in Rome, and it contains 134 columns. These vast pillars made a strong impression on Francis Frith: 'The effect which the builders appear to have had in view in this remarkable crowding together of enormous columns, is the combined impression of vastness and power – almost of awe – which they produce upon the mind when standing amongst them.' (This court is seen in pictures 1880, page 133 and 1887, page 134).

THEBES, *The Obelisk and the Granite Lotus Column c1857* 1871E

'The Lotus Column is an exquisite piece of work; the long slender stalk, and graceful flower of the lotus, were favourite architectural ornaments of the ancient Egyptians ...'

from **FRANCIS FRITH'S NOTES TO PHOTOGRAPH 1871E**

Photograph 1871E (left) was taken south-east of the obelisk from just outside the ruined walls of the inner sanctuary of Amun built by Philip Arrhidaeus (323–317BC), the successor to Alexander the Great; its remains can be seen in the right foreground. Next to this are the remains of a granite pillar with a lotus design on one face, one of a pair. The two pillars symbolised Upper and Lower Egypt. The obelisk is one of a pair that was erected by Queen Hatshepsut. It still stands, but the other was felled by an earthquake.

Today the gate in photograph 1876 (opposite) marks the end of a line of sphinxes that stretches towards the temple of Mut (the consort of Amun) and then on towards the Luxor temple. It is part of a wall built around the temple area that does not seem to have existed in Frith's day. The gate is the propylon gate of the temple of Khonsu, a temple dedicated to the worship of the son of Amun. The temple was begun by Rameses III, but not finished until Ptolemaic times. The propylon gate was constructed by Ptolemy III.

THEBES, *The Granite Pylon c1857* 1876

'Hundreds of these beautiful sculptures now enrich the museums and private collections of Europe, but only the intelligent Egyptian traveller can fully appreciate their loss to Egypt.'

FACSIMILE REPRODUCTION OF FRANCIS FRITH'S NOTES TO PHOTOGRAPH 1876 (PREVIOUS PAGE)

THE GRANITE PYLON, &c.,

KARNAC.

IT may be well to remind the reader that the numerous and unequalled remains of antiquity known as the ruins of Karnac are portions of several temples of different periods, and covering an area of several miles in circumference. This area was once surrounded by a massive brick wall of 25 feet in thickness, according to Diodorus, into which were built a number of stately and elaborately sculptured gateways and pylons. These were approached from the outward by long avenues of colossal sphynxes—not one of which, however, now remains in a perfect state; indeed, not one, I believe, now retains the head—which was that of a ram. We have already described one of those avenues, and its beautiful Ptolemaic gateway; but the present view represents an older, more massive, but less elegant and less elaborately sculptured, edifice, which I have called the Granite Pylon, in consequence of its being, as I believe, the only existing extensive pylon-gateway constructed solely of that material. I think, too, that this was the principal entrance to the sacred enclosure as it was approached from Luxor, and consequently it was from this point that the greatest of the sphynx-avenues led to the city of Thebes (Luxor), a distance of at least a mile and a half. On the outer side of this pylon I traced for a considerable distance into the cultivated land the mutilated and almost buried forms of these prodigious figures, which, as far as I recollect, were not more than eight or ten feet apart, so that this avenue alone must have consisted of more than a thousand sphynxes! The lintel-stones of this pylon deserve especial notice from their magnitude, being each a single block of granite. The sculptures represent offerings by the king to various deities—especially to the god Khan, or Khem.

On each side of the doorway is seen a colossal statue, now headless and otherwise greatly mutilated, and half buried in the *debris* of the pylon and adjoining walls. These figures are of alabaster, and are wrought and polished with the most consummate art. I may here remark, that I believe there is not now known to exist in Egypt a single statue or sphynx of movable proportions which is in any tolerable state of preservation. What can we think of a government which has systematically authorized travellers of all nations to mutilate or carry off its proudest specimens of ancient art?—an irreparable injury, which can indicate only the most barbarous carelessness of these unique treasures. Hundreds of these beautiful sculptures now enrich the museums and private collections of all Europe, but only the intelligent Egyptian traveller can fully appreciate their loss *to Egypt*. Methinks it were better that a *few* men who will be at the pains of seeking them in their legitimate places should enjoy them as they can only *there* be enjoyed, rather than that the hordes of careless people who throng the British Museum even should smile thoughtlessly at their incongruous quaintness, and, in England, their unintelligible grandeur.

Photograph 1877 (left) is of great interest to a visitor to modern Karnak, as the scene has changed so much. What immediately strikes us is the vast confusion of rubble and fallen columns lying like overturned piles of coins in the foreground. We are looking along the main axis of the Amun temple from what is now called the First Court.

As far as we can see is a scene of devastation. The main pillar in the centre right of the picture is all that remains of the Kiosk of Taharqa, one of the Nubian kings of the 25th dynasty. The main pylon gate in the picture is the second pylon, which dates to the time of Seti I, but whose decoration is Ptolemaic. Today, the court is cleared of everything but tourists.

THEBES, *The Court of Shishak c1857* 1877

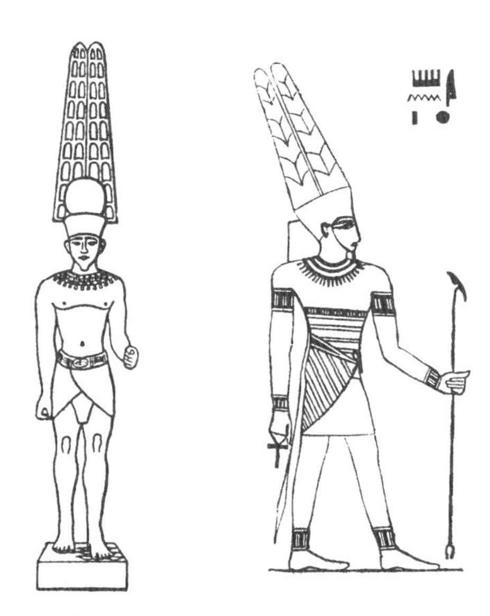

ABOVE: *Forms of Amun-Re, to whom the Court of Shishak is dedicated.*

The complex at Karnak (photograph 1883, above left) contains not just temples of Amun, but of the triad of the Amun family: Amun himself, Mut his wife, and their son Khonsu. The temple of Mut lies to the south-west of the main site, towards the modern town of Luxor, while the temple to Khonsu lies within the sanctuary of the main complex. This gate, built by Ptolemy III, belongs to Khonsu's temple. The temple proper can be seen beyond this propylon. The temple was begun by Rameses III and completed under a series of later kings, including some of the priest kings of Karnak, who ruled in the late New Kingdom and the third intermediate period. This area of the complex provided David Roberts with several views, which may have led Frith to photograph it.

View 1860 (below left), as Frith points out in his commentary, shows the top two-thirds of the columns of the Hypostyle Hall. The vast accumulation of debris evident in the picture has now been cleared, and the haphazard repairs to the columns have been rectified.

Again, for anyone who has visited Karnak photograph 1880 (opposite) is amazing. We are nearly level with the top of some of the great columns of the Hypostyle Hall. This view would be impossible today, as the debris has been cleared. Contemporary paintings show that the outer columns were indeed mostly buried in Frith's time.

ABOVE LEFT: THEBES, *A Sculptured Gateway c1857* 1883

BELOW LEFT: THEBES, *The Hall of Columns c1857* 1860

THEBES, *Pillars in the Great Hall c1857* 1880

THEBES, *The Hall of Columns, the Interior c1859* 1887

It was not until Frith's second trip to Egypt that he had perfected his photographic technique so as to be able to take a picture amongst the tumble of the interior of the Hall of Columns. The subdued light would have increased the exposure time, which although short by the standards of the time, would seem very long to us. Frith also bemoans the fact that he could give no idea of the size of the hall through either a picture or through words: 'It is perfectly hopeless to do it justice either by the camera or the pen.' Even today, it is an almost impossible place to take a successful picture.

In this view we see some of the immense columns inscribed with the deep-cut hieroglyphs that exemplify the style of Rameses II along with the open papyrus-headed columns of the central aisle in the hall.

At the top in the centre we can see the window through which sunlight would have shone in narrow beams into the interior of the temple. The grille construction was common in ancient Egypt.

THEBES, A *Hall of the Palace at Karnak* (FROM AN ENGRAVING)

Francis Frith's Notes to Photograph 1887

Before I ascended the Nile, a photographic friend, whom I met at Cairo, discouraged me greatly about Karnac. The place, he said, was impregnable – that it was idle to plant a camera against it – such vast and shapeless masses or ruin packed together as tight as it would stow, and built in on all sides with tremendous blank walls. I say I was discouraged; nevertheless, I brought up my artillery boldly, and fired away right and left – with what success I leave my readers to judge – and yet I think my friend's representations must have somewhat unmanned me; for on my first journey I attempted no interior view of the great hall, which is the chief ornament and wonder of Karnac, and indeed of Egypt. On the contrary, I wrote that 'the pillars are so strangely crowded together, and their height is so great, as to render it quite impossible to obtain a photograph within the hall itself!' But if the reader will turn back he will find that I crept around the outer wall, and took advantage of dilapidations therein effected by some former warrior, obtaining a shot across the hall, which was not altogether ineffective. And whilst the reader is there, he may perhaps like to revise what is said about this great hall. Think of the dimensions – 350 feet long, by 150. One hundred and thirty-four columns, such as are here represented, still standing. The centre avenue 75 feet high, and 36 feet in circumference. Why, there is many a snug little sitting room not more than 12 feet square: the base of one of these columns would not stand in its area! Well, on my late journey I seem to have recovered my self-possession. But I will relate how, step-by-step, I forced the enemy's positions. First, as my cavalcade of donkeys and Arabs (designedly so placed gentle reader) pattered along from Luxor in a whirlwind of dust, I sounded a hasty 'halt!' as we neared the beautiful pylon gateway of the Ptolemaic period, and although by no means regardless of the grim old sphynxes that guard it, I planted my engines, and 'took the approaches'. Then I entered the sacred enclosure, turned sharp round to the right, and carried off the pair of huge fellows who flank the remains of the glorious 'Granite Pylon'. Wheeling round my tackle, I possessed myself of an extent of the most deplorably ruinous territory that the world knows, and then I approached the enemy's stronghold – that great centre of temples and shrines, whose nucleus was formed nearly 4000 years ago, and to which a period of twenty centuries added its industry and wealth. Passing under the great unfinished pylon, I entered the 'Court of Shishak', and welcomed into the fore-ground of my picture those cheese-like piles of prostrate column-stones, which have been the delight of artists from time immemorial, but which the enlightened governor of Egypt has lately entirely swept away, that he might have a clear carriage-drive through the temple! Then, burning with ambition – yet with much fearfulness – I entered that dark vista which you see in the centre of my last picture, and turning down one of the side aisles, I pointed my camera at a double line of those dingy old immensities – indestructible – indescribable, and hitherto deemed impossible! Not so!

THEBES, *The Broken Obelisk c1857* 1896

Located to the rear of the Hypostyle Hall towards the sanctuary, this fallen obelisk (1896, above) is one of a pair originally erected by the female pharaoh Hatshepsut – she put up four obelisks in all. This one is carved with images of her coronation and a text justifying her unusual reign, as she was one of only a very few female pharaohs. This view was popular with artists, and is the subject of a sketch by Roberts. Frith includes human figures; as well as giving some indication of scale, they also echo Roberts's picture. The European figure is probably Frith's technical companion, Francis Wenham. A fascination with the signs of the fall of the ancient Egyptian civilisation is evident in much of the writing and visual art by Victorians who visited the ancient world.

THEBES, *The Entrance to the Great Temple c1857* 1869E (DETAIL)

The temple of Luxor, which lies today by the banks of the Nile more or less in the centre of the tourist-dominated town of Luxor, was begun in the reign of Amenhotep III, whose long reign fell in the middle of the 14th century BC.

The temple may have had antecedents before that time, as a small chapel dates from the time of Hatshepsut (1473–1458BC). It was built to house an aspect of the god Amun, as a fertility god: Amenemope, or Amun of the Opet festival. It also honoured Mut and Khonsu.

The Opet festival became the major religious festival in the New Kingdom, and by the time of Rameses II lasted about a month. It was linked to the Nile flood, and began in the second month of Akhet, or the rising of the waters. The god's sacred boat, carrying the sacred image, was brought by water from Karnak to Luxor Temple amid much dancing and celebration. Here the statue of the god remained, and perhaps symbolically renewed Amun's power. The king was also involved in the rites, and the festival may have been a way of the reaffirming his divine right to rule. There are scenes of this important festival inscribed high on the walls of the outer court of the temple which date from the reign of Tutankhamun.

What is especially interesting about this temple is the fact that a continuity of worship can be traced back for about 3,500 years. When paganism was replaced by Christianity during the late Roman Empire, the temple was used as the site of several small churches. When Christianity gave way to Islam, a mosque was built on the site, the mosque of Abu el-Haggag, which is still in use today.

THEBES, *The Luxor Temple 2004* T323009K

Frith's view (1869E, opposite) shows the entrance to the temple with the heads of two colossi of Rameses II sticking out of the accumulated sand and silt. Behind is the pylon gate that the same king built with images of the battle of Kadesh. Today the ground level is 20 to 30 feet lower. This has the interesting effect of suspending the mosque in the picture (the mosque of Abu el-Haggag) high above the courtyard of the temple.

In view 1870 (overleaf) we see the tops of some great columns rising above the sand. These are part of the central colonnade begun by Tutankhamun and finished by the pharaoh Horemheb. They provided a processional route for the barque of Amun in front of the temple proper during the Opet festival.

THEBES, *View at Luxor c1857* 1870E

VIEW AT LUXOR.

LUXOR, reader, is at Thebes; and Thebes, I need hardly say, is an ever present idea with the Nile traveller, from the time that his dahibieh floats out into the broad river from the dirty crowded shore of Boulac, the port of Cairo: and as you listlessly watch the lazy tramp of your sailors, as day after day they "track" your boat in the calm hot weather, or fly before the brisk north winds, your fancy has abundant opportunity for speculation on the history of this mysterious city of the past—its

"Temples, palaces, and piles stupendous,
Of which the very ruins are tremendous."

Thebes was the ancient capital of Upper Egypt; and the groups of antiquities here scattered over a large district, on both sides of the river, are of greater variety and interest than at any other single spot in Egypt. We shall have abundant opportunity, in describing succeeding views, to speak of the history and present aspects of its several divisions: in the meantime we give a map of the district, which will be useful throughout for reference.

THEBES, *Entrance into the Palace at Luxor*
(FROM AN ENGRAVING)

FACSIMILE REPRODUCTION OF FRANCIS FRITH'S NOTES TO PHOTOGRAPH 1870 (OPPOSITE)

DENDERA, *The Portico of the Temple c1857* 1902

DENDERA *2004* D239001K

Dendera is one of the more complete and one of the last temples of ancient Egypt. As Frith mentions, parts of its fascination are the Hathor-headed columns in the pronaos, which date from the age of Tiberius, and the astronomical ceiling in a roof chapel. The original was removed to the Louvre in 1823, and what we see now is a copy.

The temple site shows traces of buildings dating back to the Old Kingdom, or the time of the pyramids, whilst the main structure was largely built by Ptolemy XII Auletes in 54 BC, some two thousand years after the earliest buildings.

Frith's view echoes a painting by David Roberts, 'The Temple of Dendera, Upper Egypt' (1841), although his view is more face-on to the columns. The engraving shows that some colour remained.

FRANCIS FRITH'S NOTES TO PHOTOGRAPH 1902

Dendera is the first temple ruins which the traveller sees on his way up to Thebes. It is very imposing; and it enjoys two or three notable advantages over many other of the celebrities of the Nile valley. In the first place the locale is forsaken by the peasantry, and one can explore and admire without being subjected to the odious concomitants of Arab filth and Arab impertinence. Secondly, the ruin having been early buried in the debris of the old town, and lately cleared by Ibrahim Pacha, it is the most completely exposed and the most perfect ruin of the series ... We thought the effect of the interior view of the Portico was one of the loftiest and deepest character, little inferior to anything else in Egypt.

The one thing to be lamented, is the early Christian defacement of the capitals which represented Athor or Isis, to whom the temple was dedicated. These heads are, I believe, all of them more or less destroyed. Scarcely half of the height of the columns of the Portico is seen in my view, which was necessarily taken from the outside ... But the most interesting objects of all at Dendera are the richly coloured astronomical representations upon the ceiling of the Portico. Prominent among these is the zodiac, which afforded the French savans of Napoleon the presumptive evidence of the incorrectness of the usually received Biblical chronology. One philosopher 'fixed' the date of the inscribed zodiac at 4,000 years at the lowest computation, and a similar one at Esneh was 'proved' to date from 17,000 years B.C.

This photograph was published in the fourth instalment of the second collection of Frith's work, with a commentary by Sophia and Reginald Poole. In the distance is the unmistakable shape of the Bent Pyramid. This was constructed for the pharaoh Snefru (2613–2589BC, father of Khufu, the builder of the Great Pyramid). It was abandoned with no burial having taken place within it. A little further to the north, out of the picture, lies the Red Pyramid, which was Snefru's final resting place. In the foreground lie the remains of the pyramid of Amenemhet III (1855–1808BC). This was abandoned after the building began to collapse into the ground, causing large cracks to appear in the burial chamber. This king was eventually buried at Hawara. In excavations at this site (a report on them was published by Jacques De Morgan in 1894), the burial of a lesser-known king, Auibre-Hor, was found.

THE PYRAMIDS OF DAHSHOOR, *From the East c1857* 645

from FRANCIS FRITH'S NOTES TO PHOTOGRAPH 645

'It is a picturesque mass, of very irregular form, rising out of a mound made by its own ruins. The peasants have quarried it for building materials, and given it the rugged shape it now wears. We can scarcely regret their barbarism, which has varied the aspect of what must have long been a mere rounded Pyramid, and produced these admirable contrasts of light and shade, and of rough and smooth surface. It is built of unburnt brick, and was originally cased with stone, which appears to have been the uniform practice with brick Pyramids. The external appearance of all Pyramids seems to have been the same.' They were constructed in three principal ways: some were built with hewn blocks of stone, others were of rubble-work, kept together by stone walls, and others again of crude brick.

Today the Dahshur site (Frith's Dashoor), less visited, and further out in the desert, captures something of the mystery and remoteness of the romantic idea of the pyramid. My memory of visiting the site is the welcome and the glass of mint tea we obtained from the guardian sitting on a crimson carpet under an awning in the desert.

The Pyramids of Sakkarah (Saqqara), *From the North East c1857* 646

'... There, in the foreground, is a human skull, and a little beyond it the skull of a sacred bull. It is no unusual chance that brings them here: throughout the whole vast Necropolis the bones of men and of bulls and ibises are strewn around the mouths of the desecrated pits. The vast abundance of the remains of human mummies attests the ancient populousness of Egypt, and the length of time for which this was a favourite burial place.'

Sophia and Reginald Poole's Notes to Photograph 646
(previous page)

The view comprises the Pyramid of Steps, and another pyramid to the north-east of it. Both are admirably presented, the regular masonry of the one contrasting with the rubble of the other. The distance of the larger of the structures, the dazzling sunlight, and as strong shade on both, the undulations of shifting sand, with here and there a mummy-pit, into which an unwary passenger may easily fall, bring back to the mind every characteristic of this striking view. The lesser features are not wanting to render it complete: there, in the foreground, is a human skull, and a little beyond it the skull of a sacred bull. It is no unusual chance that brings them here: throughout the whole vast Necropolis the bones of men and of bulls and ibises are strewn around the mouths of the desecrated pits. The vast abundance of the remains of human mummies attests the ancient populousness of Egypt, and the length of time for which this was a favourite burial place.

The Pyramid of Steps is of smaller dimensions than the spectator would suppose, its position on an eminence about 90 feet above the plain, and the manner in which the pyramidal form is broken, giving it an advantage over most of the other pyramids. The present perpendicular height, according to Mr. Perring's measurement, is about 196 feet 6 inches; and the original base, on the north and south sides, was 351 feet 2 inches, and, on the east and west sides, 393 feet 11 inches. It is, as the author just mentioned observes, the only pyramid in Egypt the sides of which do not exactely face the cardinal points, the north side being 4o 35' east of the true north in its direction. The interior is very remarkable. The more ancient part consists of an inclined passage, leading to a narrow and lofty chamber, connected with small apartments. One of these is beneath the great chamber, and is entered by the roof through an aperture which was closed by a block of granite resembling the stopper of a bottle. A passage from the south-east angle of the great chamber leads to small rooms, round the doorway of one of which was a hieroglyphic inscription, which has been removed, and is now in the Berlin Museum. It comprises the name and titles of an ancient king, Ra-nub-rekhee, or Nub-rekhee-ra, not enclosed as usual in an oval ring, but followed by a circular ring, as a determinative sign. The determiative signs, it may be observed, are representations (ideographs) used to determine the sense of words written phonetically.

This inscription shews the origin of the practice of placing the royal names in oval rings, and is probably of the remotest period, before that practice was introduced. The king may not improbably be the Necherophes, or Necherochis, of Manetho, chief of his Third Dynasty, whose accession may be placed about B.C. 2650. The exceptional direction of the pyramid, its irregular dimensions, and the very archaic character of this inscription, make this by no means an unreasonable conjecture. Besides these passages and chambers, there are beneath the pyramid a gallery and numerous passages of a much later date, showing that the monument was appropriated as a place of sepulture long after its foundation, but yet in ancient times. A great period must have elapsed before a royal tomb could have been so diverted from its original use.

SAKKARAH (SAQQARA), *The Step Pyramid of Usakhaf 2004* S737001K

The fine photograph 646 (page 143) appeared in the second selection of three photographs in the second collection published in 1860 and 1862. The accompanying text was written by Sophia and Reginald Poole. We see the Step Pyramid of King Djoser (2667–2648BC), which lies on the Saqqara plateau. It is the world's first completely stone-built monument, and dates from around 2650 BC. It was built by the architect Imhotep. In the photograph the pyramid is surrounded by a sea of sand, whereas today, thanks largely to the lifelong work of the French archaeologist Jean-Philippe Lauer, the entire complex can be seen. This site demonstrates the ancient Egyptians' interest in their own past, for here we can see graffiti from a New Kingdom 'tourist', made when the complex was already nearly 1400 years old: 'The scribe Ahmose came to see the Temple of Djoser. He found it as if heaven were within it, Ra rising in it ...' (see also page 8). In the foreground we can see the remains of the pyramid of Userkhaf (2494–2487BC), an early fifth dynasty pharaoh.

GEEZEH (GIZA), *The Sphynx and the Great Pyramid c1857* 643

View 643 (page 146) was taken from the south-east, looking towards the side of the pyramid that is now the home of the Solar Boat museum. In the foreground is a splendid image of the Sphinx, buried up to its shoulders in sand. This is very similar to many views painted at roughly the same time. 'The Pyramids', for example, exhibited in London by William James Müller in the 1840s, was painted from almost the same spot. The Sphinx was a huge sculpture for King Khafre (2520–2494BC), and is almost certainly a portrait of him. In later times it was linked to the god of the rising sun, Re-Horakhty. The pharaoh Tuthmosis IV (1401–1391BC) conducted the first excavation of the monument, and erected a stele between the paws of the giant lion. The stele tells how Tuthmosis found the statue buried in sand, and after a dream foretelling his becoming king, had it cleared. The Great Pyramid in the background was built by workers under Khafre's father, Khufu (2551–2528BC). Until the Eiffel Tower was built, it was the tallest structure on Earth. It remains the only one of the ancient wonders of the world still standing.

'The day and hour in a man's life upon which he first obtains a view of the Pyramids is a time to date from for many years to come; he is approaching, as it were, the presence of an immortality which has mingled vaguely with his thoughts from very childhood ...'

TOP: GEEZEH (GIZA), *The Sphinx and Khufu's Pyramid 2004* G318001K
ABOVE: GEEZEH (GIZA), *Khufu's Pyramid 2004* G318004K

GIZA, *The Pyramids c1857* 642E

View 642E (opposite) has become the iconic image of the pyramids, one that camel drivers today encourage tourists to take after a ride on their camels. Frith's photograph was included in the first selection published in 1860. In the foreground a figure reclines on the dune gazing at the pyramids. As well as giving us an idea of the scale of the monuments, this figure suggests the romance of the setting.

The photograph shows the three satellite pyramids of Menkaure. The straight-sided one, almost disappearing into the bulk of the King's tomb, is the cult pyramid. The two step pyramids are the Queen's pyramids. A cult pyramid occurs in all pyramid complexes after Sneferu, but its function is debated. It could have had the same ritual function as the south tomb found at Saqqara: a housing for the king's entrails in canopic jars – or a cenotaph or memorial to the king. It might have been used to house the ka statue of the king, a statue to allow the ka or soul of the king to have a home after the death of the king. As neither of the so-called Queen's pyramids is named, there is some doubt whether they belonged to any of Menkaure's queens (2490–2472BC).

Behind these stands the pyramid of Menkaure. This king had a long and peaceful reign. He was the son of Khafre, in the shadow of whose pyramid his stands. Khafre's pyramid is the middle of the three great pyramids, and still retains some of the original casing at the apex. Behind it is the pyramid of Khufu, the largest of the three.

For a modern visitor to Egypt 1901E (above right) is a remarkable photograph. Firstly, the growth of Cairo in the 20th century makes the repetition of the image impossible. What we see here now lies under the sprawl of the modern city. Secondly, the clarity of the air is something that the pollution of the modern city has destroyed. Thirdly, the picture has been taken during the inundation, the annual summer flooding of the river, that has been stopped by the building of the Aswan High Dam. In the far distance we see the flood plain covered with water gently shining in the sun, an image familiar to the ancients but lost to us.

THE NILE, *From the Quarries at Toura c1857* 1901E

From these quarries at Toura the Egyptians used to obtain the fine white limestone they used as casing for the pyramids. Only the second pyramid at Giza and the Bent Pyramid at Dashur still have any casing left on them.

CAIRO, *Street View c1857* 1929

For visitors in the 19th century, Cairo seems to have been a distillation of the excitements and frustrations they found in the rest of the country. For some, the minarets and the call of the muezzin represented a half-constructed image of the orient. The Reverend A C Smith, writing in 1868, talks of the place calling up images of the 'Arabian Nights'. However, in the 'Graphic' of 18 December 1869 a square in Cairo is described as 'a dreary expanse', whilst the streets are 'not clean ... not handsome ... not convenient'. Frith's street scene (1929) tends to conceal what is not picturesque. Again, one is struck by the modernity of the rectangular buildings with their ornately carved wooden meshrebeeyas, or overhanging windows. In fact, Mohammed Ali banned these as a fire risk, although a concern to build in what he saw as a European style may have lain behind his ban. He also ordered the removal of the stone benches in front of the buildings to allow the passage of carriages. When the photograph was first published, the Pooles' commentary was perceptive: 'The street in this view gives us an idea of the repose of Eastern life in the Muslim quarters, undisturbed by association with the bustling, anxious European.' Some of Frith's images are taken from a rooftop or from high in the Citadel. The practical reason for this is because the vast throngs of people, who would have appeared as blurs on the long exposure plates, could only be avoided in this way. In some of these photographs we see strange ramp like structures, all pointing to the north (C711008, opposite) . These were an early form of air conditioning: the north is the direction from which the cooling breezes blow. It is interesting that some New Kingdom houses seem to have very similar constructions, an arrangement which stood the test of nearly four thousand years (see the house at the extreme right of ZZZ00151, opposite).

LEFT: CAIRO, *General View showing Rooftop Ventilators c1857*
C711008 (WITH DETAIL ABOVE).

BELOW: *The Papyrus of Nakht House and Garden* ZZZ00151

'[The mourners] have brought with them every luxury that their homes could spare – cushions, mattresses, prayer-carpets, and good cheer of every description suitable to the climate. The rich are attended by their slaves, and the poorer have begged and borrowed all that they require for the journey and the stay. Especially on the occasions of the two festivals, the so-called sorrowing Muslims eat, drink, and enjoy themselves during three days and nights.'

FACSIMILE REPRODUCTION OF SOPHIA AND REGINALD POOLE'S NOTES TO PHOTOGRAPH 1931E (OPPOSITE)

THE CITADEL OF CAIRO,

WITH THE MOSQUE OF MOHAMMAD 'ALEE, FROM A CEMETERY TO THE SOUTH-EAST, AT THE FOOT OF THE GEBEL EL-MUKATTAM.

THE Citadel (El-Kal'ah) was founded by Saláh-ed-Deen (Saladin), A.D. 1176-7. It overlooks Cairo from the south-east, crowning a rocky hill 250 feet above the level of the plain; and was constructed mainly of the materials of a number of small pyramids, adjacent to those which still form conspicuous, though distant objects, as seen from this elevation.

The great mosque within its walls we watched for years in its slow progress. It is the Mosque of Mohammad 'Alee; and there, by his direction, he was interred. The architecture is of a mixed character, and not rich in decoration, though the building is very costly: its columns are of alabaster, and its proportions have a certain grandeur; but the minarets, being very lofty, and peculiarly slender, produce an incongruous effect. To the right of it is the extensive ruined mosque of the Sultán Mohammad Ibn-Kala-oon, with two minarets, and the base of a dome. It was built in the early part of the fourteenth century. On the round tower, a little more to the right, may be traced a telegraph, the first of a series extending to Alexandria. Several very large palaces are included in the Citadel, together with a labyrinth of private dwellings.

The lower strata of the Mukattam range will interest the geologist, and many a powerful glass will be used to magnify the base, which, in two semicircular projections, is happily brought into the right of this view. The Gebel El-Mukattam commands the Citadel, as the latter commands Cairo. Between them runs a shallow valley, in which the most interesting objects are the cemetery in this view, and the picturesque houses and enclosures attached to it. These were erected for the accommodation of mourners who periodically pay their visits here to wail at the tombs of their relations and friends, especially on the occasions of the two Mohammadan festivals—the greater and lesser 'Eed, called by the Turks the two Beiráms,—when the cemeteries are crowded to excess, and, as the houses are private property, tents are pitched for those who do not possess them. Long trains of women and children are then seen visiting the burial-grounds, and the first impression is that it is an interesting and affecting sight, and it is natural to listen, and to hush every sound besides, that the melancholy and measured wail may be heard as it is borne upon the air. While the periodical expression of sorrow does violence to established conviction, that the anguish of bereavement belongs to no particular day, there is something in the belief that those Eastern mourners are on their way to perform pious duties which fascinates the spectator; but, if they be followed to the houses, it will be seen that, with very few exceptions, they have brought with them every luxury that their homes could spare—cushions, mattresses, prayer-carpets, and good cheer of every description suitable to the climate. The rich are attended by their slaves, and the poorer have begged and borrowed all that they require for the journey and the stay. Especially on the occasions of the two festivals, the so-called sorrowing Muslims eat, drink, and enjoy themselves during three days and nights; and they delight in unusually large gatherings, for the reason, often expressed, that the more numerous the party, the merrier are the groups assembled. The women generally take a palm-branch to break up and place on the tomb, and some cakes or bread to distribute to the poor: this is done for the sake of the dead, in whose register it is supposed to be put down by the recording angel.

CAIRO, *The Citadel c1857* 1931E

CAIRO, *The Citadel Gateway c1857* 2813

The Citadel still dominates part of the Cairo skyline, although the view in 1931E would simply be impossible to see today. The sprawl of the city has covered all the area around the rock on which the Citadel is built. It has been occupied since AD 810, and it was first fortified by Salah-a-din (Saladin) in 1176. The mosque of Mohammed Ali, which dominates the view, would have been very new when Frith took his photograph – it was constructed between 1830 and 1857. The Citadel gate picture shows the Bab el-Azab, which was built by Abd el-Rahman Katkhuda in 1754. Today the gate has been tidied up and by-passed – the main entrance to the Citadel complex today is via the north or south gates.

CAIRO, *The Citadel Gate 2004* C711004K

'The Rumeyleh is the scene of fairs, as it was formerly of races and other games. The horse-market of Cairo is held in it, and in this view are seen some of the horses picketted in a row, forming part of the fair ... The Rumeyleh is also the principal place of execution of Muslims convicted of capital offences.'

from **FRITH'S NOTES TO PHOTOGRAPH 2813**
(opposite)

Of all the places photographed by Frith, it is arguable that Cairo has undergone the most obvious changes. The photograph taken from the Southern Cemetery (1966, overleaf) shows a wide expanse of sand at a short distance from the Citadel. As the city has grown (it now has a population of roughly 17 million, more than twice the size of London), so all traces of open land have been submerged. The position that Frith used for this shot would, I estimate, be somewhere in the middle of the six-lane Cairo ring road today. In their description of the view of the Southern Cemetery, the Pooles mention how citizens of Cairo lived in the 'excellence of the pavilions'. This Cairene tradition, dating back to the 14th century, still continues today: in 1980 the living population of these cemeteries was 25,000 people.

CAIRO, *Tombs in the Southern Cemetery c1857* 1966

CAIRO, *The Ezbekeeya c1857* 1927

The view of the Ezbekeeya (1927, previous page) is in sharp contrast to the dwellings in the cemetery (1966, page 156). The Ezbekeeya was a fashionable area for many years. It originally lay on the banks of a lake; but by the time that Frith visited this had been filled in for twenty years, although a building programme by Mohammed Ali in a more modern style, and the location of one of his own palaces here, still allowed the area to have social cachet. It was also the site of the first European-style hotels in Egypt, including the very first, the Hotel Giardino; also here were the Hotel du Nil, which was visited by Flaubert in 1849–50, and the New British Hotel, which became the famous Shepheard's. What is striking about the image is the very modern appearance of the buildings. However, the roofline of the third building from the right shows signs of an ancient influence: it has a cavetto cornice, similar to those on some temples, such as the ones at Dendera and Kom Ombo.

Sophia and Reginald Poole's Notes to Photograph 1927 *(previous page)*

In the north-west quarter of the city is a large irregular tract, called the 'Ezbekeeyah', or 'Birket El-Ezbekeeyeh', named after the Emeer El-Ezbekee. It is nearly half a mile long, and about a third of a mile broad at its widest extent. The scene here represented is well-known to European travellers, being a portion of a row of lofty houses bounding it on the north-east, and forming part of the south-western side of the great Coptic Quarter, which covers a considerable space behind. On the extreme left is the entrance to a little quarter, called the 'Radwaneeyeh', and beyond it was the Bab-el-Hadeed, built by Salah-ed-Deen (Saladin), a gate taken down some years since, the neighbourhood of the site of which is now the scene of the noise and bustle of a railway terminus.

On the south of the Ezbekeeyeh are two Turkish palaces, modern in their architecture, and standing in gardens. On the west is a long plain wall (now forming part of th city-wall), and another Turkish palace, the house of the famous and unfortunate Memlook Bey El-Elfee. It became the residence of Napoleon during the French occupation, and subsequently of his general, Kleber, who was assassinated in an adjacent garden. The notorious Mohammad Bey Deftardar afterwards resided in that palace; and dark and dreadful is the history of his cruelties within its walls, and in the public exercise of his functions as Registrar-general of Finance. Perhaps a more detestable monster never existed. He revelled in inflicting barbarous punishments; and his own servants frequently, though unsuccessfully, attempted his life: but he was a man of considerable ability, and is said generally to have made a show of justice in the horrible acts of which he was guilty. Adjoining this palace is the principal and well-conducted English hotel. It was formerly used as a school of languages.

CAIRO, *The Mosque of Kaitbey c1857* 1930E

Picture 1930E (previous page) shows an image of the Mosque of Kaitbey. This mosque appears on the Egyptian one pound note; its slim minaret is a beautiful and elegant structure. It stands in the Northern Cemetery, and is part of a burial assemblage which dates back to the Mausoleum of Princess Tughay (1348). The foreground of the photograph is dominated by ruins, but the dome of the mosque and its slim minaret are clearly visible.

The photograph of the Mosque of the Emeer Akhoor (648E, right) shows a somewhat dilapidated image of Cairo, in common with many of the pictures that Frith took. Today that image is far from the truth. When one is taking pictures in modern Cairo, the main problem is the traffic: modern Toyotas and Mercedes jostle with rather less well-maintained black and white Peugeot taxis. People wave and are genuinely delighted that a visitor has visited some of the more modern Muslim monuments of the city. Everyone knows where a particular mosque is, but often it still remains elusive in the tangle of streets.

Frith's Notes to Photograph 648E *(opposite)*

The Mosque of the Emeer Akhor (in Cairo commonly pronounced 'Yakhoor') stands a little to the north-east of the great square called the Rumeyleh, which is between the Citadel and the Mosque of the Sultan Hasan. It is one of the best examples of the Mosque architecture of the period of the Circassian Memlook Sultans, commencing a little before, and ending a little after, the fifteenth century. It must not be confounded with a mosque bearing the same name, but also called the Nasireeyeh, near one of the western gates of the city called by the latter name.

No one who can be touched by grandeur of form, symmetry of proportion, and extraordinary harmony of effect, and who has enjoyed the perfect combination of these qualities in one view of Cairo, commanding her almost countless domes and minarets (the mosques being more than two hundred and fifty in number), will fail to record that privilege with the deep feeling of first and fresh impressions; for, in all that is most striking and interesting, Cairo is unlike any other city in the world. The mosques are its most characteristic objects, and exhibit every beauty of the Alhambra, with far greater elegance and purity both in the details and in the general forms. But their architecture displays considerable variety, commencing with the grand and massive style of Ibn-Toolon and El-Hakim, and gradually assuming lighter forms in the age of the Memlook Sultans.

'Cairo is unlike any other city in the world. The mosques are its most characteristic objects, and exhibit every beauty of the Alhambra, with far greater elegance and purity both in the details and in the general forms.'

CAIRO, *The Mosque of Emeer Akhoor c1857* 648E

CAIRO, *The Mosque of El-Hakim c1857* 656

'It is melancholy to see the tottering and rent structures, of surpassing beauty of detail and form, in and around Cairo which have suffered from such causes. During less than eight years, we experienced three earthquakes, and seventy houses fell in the one fearful shock of the last and most tremendous of those three visitations, all of which were sufficiently alarming.'

Sophia and Reginald Poole's Notes to Photograph 656 *(previous page)*

The mosque in which this view is taken is rendered extremely interesting by its antiquity, by the style of its architecture, and by the infamous character of the khaleefeh whose name it bears; a wretch who professed himself a prophet, and even, at length, to be God incarnate.

This remarkable monument was founded by the Khaleefeh El-Ajeez, the father of the Khallefeh El-Hakim, who completed it in the year of the Flight 403, A.D. 1012–13. It is situated immediately within that portion of the northern wall of Cairo which connects the two great city-gates, called Bab en-Nasr and Bab el-Futooh. The space which it occupies is almost an exact square, of which each side measures little less than 400 feet. With the exception of one other mosque (that of Ibn-Toolon, which very little exceeds it in size), it is the largest in Cairo. It consists of porticoes surrounding a spacious square court open to the sky. The portico on the south-east (that is, the side towards Mekkeh) had four rows of columns, that on the south-west three, and each of the other porticoes two. At the northern angle, which is that seen in our view, is a massive tower (partly concealed in that view) supporting a mad'neh, or minaret; and at the western angle is a similar tower, with a similar mad'neh. It is stated that both these mad'nehs were partly thrown down by an earthquake; and it is said that, though repaired, they are not what they originally were in height nor in form. The arches are very beautiful in their curves, and slightly pointed, like those of the Mosque of Ibn-Toolon, which is more than a hundred years older, and about three hundred years anterior to the period when the pointed arch is said to have been first introduced into England.

A scene of deplorable desolation presents itself to the visitor on his entering the Mosque, which is no longer used as a place of worship. On every side he sees crumbling ruins, and pillars that supported arches sustaining only remnants of the superstructure. Considering the massive and compact character of this great edifce, its demolition can only be accounted for by the occurrence of frequent shocks of earthquakes, before the year 1507, when the Sultan Beybars repaired it. It is rarely found that even the most careful restoration gives the original solidity to a building which has been once shattered by such a convulsion. It is melancholy to see the tottering and rent structures, of surpassing beauty of detail and form, in and around Cairo which have suffered from such causes. During less than eight years, we experienced three earthquakes, and seventy houses fell in the one fearful shock of the last and most tremendous of those three visitations, all of which were sufficiently alarming.

A common thoroughfare passes through the Mosque, from the middle of the north-west side, to the middle of the side opposite. Over the north-west entrance is a remarkable inscription in the Koofee (or Cufic) character, mentioned by Sir Gardner Wilkinson, who has published a transcript of the most important portion of it. The following is a translation: – 'El-Hakim-bi-amri-llah, Prince of the Faithful: the blessings of God be on him, and on his pure ancestors. In the month of Regeb, the year three and ninety and three hundred'.

The date of this inscription (corresponding to A.D. 1003) shows that it was executed about nine years before the completion of the Mosque. But what is most worthy of notice in it is the fact that it records the assumption of El-Hakim to himself of the dignity of a prophet – for the phrase 'upon whom be the blessings of God' is applied by the Muslims peculiarly to prophets and apostles.

The interior of the Mosque is ornamented with numerous inscriptions of passages from the Kur-an, also in the ancient character termed Koofee, and executed in stucco. Three portions of these inscriptions are seen in the view which we are describing; two of them are but very small fragments, affording no complete sense. The third, which is of a somewhat later style (a flexuous kind of Kufee), contains the last letter of the ninth verse of the eighth chapter of the Kur-an, and the greater portion of the next verse, which we thus translate, enclosing between brackets the concluding words of the verse, which are not comprised in the view: – 'And God appointed it not save as good tidings for you, and in order that your hearts might be set at ease thereby: and victory is not save from God: verily God is mighty (and) wise.' Here it may be mentioned that what is rendered 'for you', is not in the received text of the Kur-an.

CAIRO, *From the East c1857* 649

FRITH'S NOTES TO PHOTOGRAPH 649 (OPPOSITE)

The general view over the city is highly illustrative of the aspect of Cairo. There are the clustering domes, no less than five, immediately before the spectator, with four mosques (for there is a small old minaret on the right), and in the distance, the domes and minarets are almost countless. In front of the principal mosque stands one of those quaint prison-like houses that, in a house-top view, here and there over-top their lesser neighbours, and by their dismal ugliness, call to mind, first of all, the many crimes that may have been commtted within them. Yet these houses, on the side next the main street are generally ornamented with the beautiful projecting windows of lattice-work, and we think, with Mr. Monckton Miles, of the 'Thousand and One Nights', and 'concealed jewels', lutes, and carousals. And if we are fortunate enough to penetrate beyond the crooked passage of the door – always crooked, that no one may uninvited see beyond a few feet from the entrance, to disturb the privacy of the inmates – a cheerful, swept, and watered courtyard, with spacious arched and open-fronted reception rooms for male guests, generally surprises us; and yet again, beyond that court, there is, perhaps, one more private still – for the hareem only. Grapevines are trained over a trellis that shades the courts, and jasmine twines among them; and in the mulberry-tree, which is often planted in the courts, cooes the wild turtle-dove. An air of quiet decay makes the spectator a little melancholy, but repose is, perhaps, the uppermost mental sensation. The house that has raised this train of reflection is shut in by wretched hovels; and so such houses always are in Cairo, except in a few favoured quarters. One of these hovels is in such a state of dilapidation that we must believe it to be a 'Wakf', or building let as legacy to a mosque; all the most wretched ruins in Cairo being mosque-property.

CAIRO *2004* C711003K

CAIRO, *A Street View 2004* C711006K

CAIRO, *A Street View 2004* C711005K

CAIRO, *A Mosque Roof 2004* C711002K

CAIRO, *A Minaret at Kait Bey Mosque 2004* C711007K

The Photographs

OUT OF EGYPT

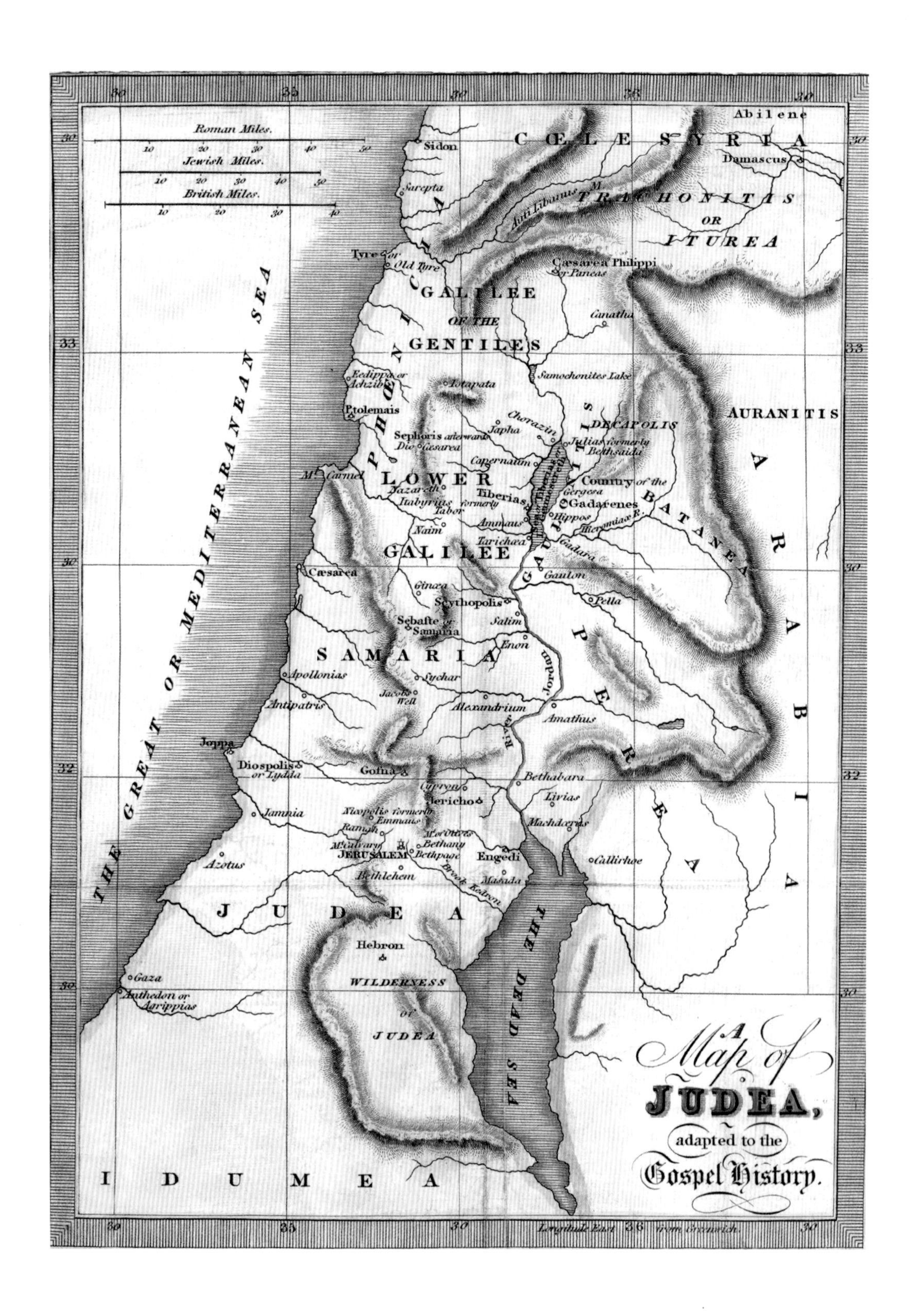

MAP OF JUDEA A001025

GAZA, *The Old Town c1860* 530E

'There is nothing more melancholy than the existence of a place, while its ancient inhabitants have become extinct. Gaza is still a city, but the Philistines have disappeared … They have utterly perished, and are as if they had never been …'

Sophia and Reginald Poole's Notes to Photograph 530E *(previous page)*

There is nothing more melancholy than the existence of a place, while its ancient inhabitants have become extinct. Gaza is still a city, but the Philistines have disappeared … They have utterly perished, and are as if they had never been … Like all Philistine towns, Gaza is pleasantly situate in a rich country, and it has gardens within and around it. The view displays this fertility in singular contrast with the ruin and desolation of the town. Many gardens may be seen, those in the foreground partly hedged with the prickly pear. The number of palms and of other trees within the walls is very unusual in an oriental town. The buildings are picturesque, without any high degree of architectural merit. The tower of the mosque to the right is, however, somewhat remarkable in its style, and, without its modern top, is superior to the usual works of Muslim architecture in Palestine. The gateway to the left of the mosque is an interesting object, with the look-out window above, and, within, the extreme darkness which is very characteristic of Eastern streets. The lantern to the left is a beautiful object, although in a very ruined state: it probably belongs to a private house.

For Frith, Gaza's association with the story of Samson was clearly of some importance when he visited it in either early 1859 or the summer of 1860. The area has other Biblical links, notably with the Philistines. Today, of course, it is part of the much disputed Palestinian Authority. The mosque in the picture of the Old Town (530E, page 169) was described by Cunningham Geikie in 1880 in his book 'The Holy Land and the Bible – A Book of Scripture Illustrations gathered in Palestine'. He describes how the building stands on a hill in the centre of the town, and how the mosque was originally a church. There had been pagan temples on the same site as well. The mosque is thus another example of the continuity with the past we meet so often.

The commentary by the Pooles for these pictures makes explicit the Biblical links; they recount the story of Samson when he pulled down the gates (the possible remains of the gates can be seen in 531E, page 171).

They also comment on the lushness of the vegetation – there is good evidence of this on the hills in the foreground of the picture.

GAZA, *Samson's Gate c1860* 531E

HEBRON *c1860* 528E

Sophia and Reginald Poole's Notes to Photograph 528E *(opposite)*

There are no roads in Palestine, but merely mule-tracks between important places – the 'beaten tracks' in which travellers have been content to follow each other from year to year, in order to 'do' Palestine. Now Hebron is the most southerly place of mark in the Holy Land. I took it from Jerusalem, returning thither after three days. Passing the tomb of Rachel – a very probable traditionary site – I encamped for the first night at Bethlehem, where I spent the best part of my time in galloping frantically round the town, in the vain search for a point of view from which I might convey to the British public something like a truthful idea of this interesting place. Leaving it in the morning, in no very appropriate frame of mind, I passed the beautiful Wady Urtas, in which Solomon's gardens were situated, and where now the small modern Jewish agricultural mind is developing itself under the patronage of a benevolent European society.

Following the lead of a stone aqueduct, I came next upon the Pools of Solomon – three magnificent tanks, which still supply Jerusalem with water, by means of the very business-like aqueduct before-named, of some eight or ten miles in length. The Pools vary from nearly 400 to 600 feet long, by 170 to 240 feet wide. They are lined throughout with excellent cement, and are in wonderful preservation. Hence succeeds a desolate and barren tract of country, until, as you approach Hebron, you come upon the roughly paved road, upon which, as my mule slipped and scrambled along, I could not help saying to myself – 'Peradventure, King David's mule hath also slipped and scrambled.'

Lord Nugent says 'The Jewish inhabitants of the place seem to be living prosperously and on good terms with the Mohammedans, and to carry on a fair trade with their own brethren and the Christians. In the adjacent parts of Judea, in earthenware and coarse cloth; wine, which is not bad; oil, which is good; a sort of ardent spirit which is detestable; and the medicine used in England for coughs under the name of paregoric elixir.'

Hebron once again is a place that has been disputed. It too lies in the Palestinian authority on the West Bank. Its importance today, as in the time of Frith, is that it is the burial place of Abraham, the patriarch venerated by Jews, Christians and Muslims. The cave of Macpelah, whose name means 'divided in two', is Abraham's burial place; it lies under the mosque, whose unusual shape can be seen at the centre top of picture 529E, page 174. The walls of this solid-looking structure are eight feet thick, and they are interspersed at regular intervals with buttresses increasing the thickness still further. The minaret of the mosque can be seen in the distance to the left rising above the bushes in picture 528E, opposite.

HEBRON, *The Mosque covering the Cave of Macpelah c1860* 529E

FRITH'S NOTES TO PHOTOGRAPH 529E *(opposite)*

We gave in our last article a description of the journey from Jerusalem to Hebron, and a sketch of the chief incidents in its ancient history. The present view is taken from the slope over against the northern portion of the town, which is partly occupied as a cemetery, and where travellers usually encamp. The houses of Hebron are of stone – lofty and tolerably well built. They have flat roofs, with the addition of one, and sometimes two, small domes – a style peculiar to Judea. Around the Great Mosque, which is conspicuous in the present View, are the bazaar and the business quarter of the town. The town is at present unwalled, but has several gates at the entrances of the principal streets. Above and around, the hills may be observed to be sprinkled over with olive trees, some of which are very old. Of the general aspect of the place, Stanley says: – 'These cultivated valleys of Hebron are hardly distinguishable (except by their olives) from the general features of a rich valley in Yorkshire or Derbyshire. The absence of palms and the presence of daisies greatly contributes to this result'. The daisies are upon Stanley's authority: I myself did not notice them. This is a true mountain valley, being, according to Russegger, 2842 (Paris) feet above the level of the sea; or, as Stanley observes, only 400 feet lower than the summit of Helvellyn.

As has been mentioned in the previous article, Hebron is the seat of several branches of manufacture, especially of small glass lamps, many of which are sent in Egypt. These glass manufactories are mentioned in the fifteenth century as flourishing at Hebron. Professor Robinson also mentions a manufactory of water skins; as many as 1500 were lying about the yard, stuffed with an infusion of oak bark. The bazaars are plentifully supplied with fruit, especially raisins; for the finest of the grapes which are grown so abundantly in the valley are dried as raisins, and the rest being trodden and pressed, the juice is boiled down to a syrup resembling molasses, which is used as a condiment with food. No wine is made, except by the Jews ...

HEBRON, *The Macpelah c2000*
BY KIND PERMISSION OF TODD BOLEN/BIBLEPLACES.COM

SINAI, *The Wadee el-Mukattab c1860* 525

'The sharp forms of the rock, the deep shade within, and the gradations of the lighter surface, with its strange Sinaitic inscriptions, are beautifully rendered ... The inscriptions often present a mixture of letters and rude representations, like the horsemen in the view, and thus almost bear the appearance of random scrawls.'

FRITH'S NOTES TO PHOTOGRAPH 525

This view represents a characteristic portion of the Wadee El-Mukattab. To the left is seen the entrance of one of the natural caves in which the district abounds, the supposed dwellings of the ancient Horim. The sharp forms of the rock, the deep shade within, and the graduations of the lighter surface, with its strange Sinaitic inscriptions, are beautifully rendered. Before the rock a group of thorny desert-shrubs grows from the sand, here almost free from the masses of stone that generally strew the surface of the desert of Sinai. In the distance is the fine mountain barrier that walls in the valley.

The Wadee el-Mukattab, or 'Inscribed Valley', takes its name from the numerous Sinaitic inscriptions which are cut upon its rocks. It branches from the Wadee Feyran, and stretches in a north-westerly direction to the Gulf of Suez, thus forming a natural approach from westward to Gebel Serbal and to Gebel Moosa, one of which must be the Sinai of Scripture. It has been, therefore, supposed that these inscriptions were cut by the Israelites during their wanderings, a conjecture which has met with some favour in England, from the

boldness with which it has been put forth, in defiance of facts and criticism. We shall endeavour, in this and subsequent descriptions, to state the chief points of evidence as to the date of the inscriptions, and to explain the theory of interpretation which sound scholars have proposed.

The Sinaitic inscriptions, although most abundant in the Wadee el-Mukattab, occur in other parts of the peninsula; and as Sir Gardner Wilkinson observes, on the authority of Dr. Ruppell, on the Egyptian shore, opposite its most southern part ('Modern Egypt and Thebes', ii. p. 385). This last fact is of the greatest importance, since it shews that the inscriptions are found where we have no reason to believe the Israelites to have been, and thus strikes at the very root of the chief argument in favour of the Israelitish origin of those in Sinai.

The inscriptions often present a mixture of letters and rude representations, like the horsemen in the view, and thus almost bear the appearance of random scrawls. Some, however, are comparatively regular, and make it certain that an alphabet is used. The forms of the letters show a strong affinity to the Himyeritic character of Southern Arabia, and other cognate early Semitic alphabets.

SINAI, *Sinaitic Inscriptions in Wadee El-Mukattab c1860* 526 (DETAILS)

SINAI, *The Summit of Gebel Moosa c1860* 527E

GEBEL (JEBEL) MUSA, *The Summit c2000*
BY KIND PERMISSION OF TODD BOLEN/BIBLEPLACES.COM

At the summit of Gebel Musa is the chapel to the Holy Trinity. This chapel was rebuilt in 1934 on the ruins of a 4th–5th century church. The interior of the chapel is decorated with frescoes from the life of Moses. Slightly to the west of the chapel is a small mosque built in the 12th century. Beneath this mosque is the traditional cave where Moses spent 40 days and where the Lord appeared to Elijah.

FRITH'S NOTES TO PHOTOGRAPH 527E

The great signs which accompanied the giving of the Law no doubt convulsed all the tract, and involved it in the same mysterious sanctity. No one can look up at these grand masses, without feeling the awfulness of the whole region. At Jerusalem, human life, and the hundred distractions, prevent our realizing the past; but here, away from the homes of men, in the desert – which always seems nearer to God than lands inhabited by man – the great events that made this holy ground are ever present to our minds.

The view is taken from the high irregular plateau from which rises the loftiest summit, 7,498 feet above the sea. The perpendicular forms of the granite of the rounded height, utterly bared by the storms, rise grandly from the base, covered, like the lower region in the foreground, with washed-down fragments. Immediately before us is a desolate tract, among the loose stones of which grow prickly desert-shrubs, the food of camels. The little tent, and the Arabs seated around it, are appropriate to the country: they are Tor Bedawees, the first genuine Arabs whom the traveller sees in the ordinary Eastern route, except between Cairo and Suez. The tribes of the desert west of Egypt are mixed with the earlier Moorish race, and those of the eastern desert are generally more of the ancient Egyptian or Ethiopian stock than of Arab origin. The Ababdeh and Bisharees indeed, especially the latter, more nearly resemble the ancient Egyptians, as represented on their monuments, than any other people, except the Nubians.

SINAI, *Mount Horeb c1860* 534

'What a grand simplicity of outline and form, filling the beholder with awe as he stands beneath, and sees the mountain rise heavenward from the plain! How must they have felt who stood here when the mountain it was death to touch burnt with fire, and the terrible sounds and sights shadowed forth the severe justice of the dispensation they announced.'

Frith's Notes to Photograph 534 *(opposite)*

The identification of the mountains and other natural features of the peninsula of Sinai mentioned in the Bible, is one of the greatest difficulties of sacred geography. We have not alone to bear in mind that there is no trustworthy local tradition to aid us, but also that there is great uncertainty as to the precise meaning of the names employed in the Scriptures. The great group of heights of the head of the peninsula appears to be called indifferently Sinai and Horeb, and these names again to be applied in the same manner to the mount from which Law was given. The name of the Mount of God seems to be also applied to this sacred height, unless, indeed, as Ritter suggests, another mountain be intended by it. In the present day, Sinai is commonly held to be that lofty ridge of granite, about three miles in length, which lies between the parallel valleys Wadee Shu'eyb and El-Leja. The northern end of this ridge is conjectured to be Horeb, and the southern, called by the Arabs Jebel Mooa, is supposed to be Sinai. These are arbitrary suppositions, but there are strong grounds for holding that the modern Horeb is the true Mount of the Law. Horeb alone, as far as observation has been carried, fulfills the requirements of the sacred narrative. It rises grandly, and at once from the great plain Er-Raha, which having a surface of full one square mile, and, including its extensions, of twice as much, is amply sufficient for the Israelite encampment. Without attempting anything like a positive decision of this much-contested point, we are of the opinion that at present the balance of probabilities is very much greatly in favour of this identification.

If this view be more than probable, how great an interest has the scene in which we may look up, as did the Israelites, to the Mount! The place is fit for the solemn event. What a grand simplicity of outline and form, filling the beholder with awe as he stands beneath, and sees the mountain rise heavenward from the plain! How must they have felt who stood here when the mountain it was death to touch burnt with fire, and the terrible sounds and sights shadowed forth the severe justice of the dispensation they announced. Even now we seem in Sinai to see the Law, noble and true, but devoid of the tenderness of the Gospel, like the vast barren mountain whence it was given to man, with no final resting-place for a human soul except in the promises of a better future. As in the Law there was this glimpse of life, so here in the valley, beneath the Mount of the Law, we see, as the symbol of the Gospel, a hospitable convent, whose garden invites the wearied eye to rest in its shade.

Would that we could again mentally people this great plain, and recall the incidents of the stay beneath the Mount. How marvellous must have been the aspect of the desert inhabited by so vast an army – those whose bones were afterwards to whiten its surface! The great wonders we dare not attempt to realize; we too may not pass the limits that have been set for us. But the lesser events would be full of interest – the noble presence of Moses and Aaron, the strange fickle people, now reverent, now disobedient, one day fearing to be near the Mount, the next making an idol to worship beneath it, while the echoes of the thunders had scarcely died away. In such views as these we rejoice that neither nature nor man can change the main features of the scene, and thus disturb our efforts to read history by the light of our own impressions.

SINAI, *The Convent and the Plain of Er-Raha c1860* 536 (DETAIL)

In the view (above right, 536) we look down the valley in which the convent stands towards the Plain of Er-Raha. The scene is strangely desolate. In the immediate foreground, up to the convent walls, stretches an arid tract strewn with broken fragments of rock, some of which are of vast size, as we see by comparing them with the little encampment in front. The fortress-like convent rises finely in the distance, and further still the Plain of Er-Raha is spread out beneath the encircling mountains, among which, to the left, in the extreme distance, may be seen the lofty ridges of Serbal. Here, as we look down on the plain, its fitness for the Israelite encampment is as evident as when we see it from the opposite direction, extending beneath the noble front of Horeb.

For Frith the attraction of Sinai, which he visited in 1860, was clearly its Biblical associations, and in the case of the image of the Convent of Sinai (536, page 182), its association with the early days of Christianity. However, the composition of these images seems to derive from the interest among artists of the day in rendering an exact copy of the landscape, 'rejecting nothing, selecting nothing, and scorning nothing', in the words of Ruskin. In 1855 an article in the 'Art Journal' was published entitled 'Geology: its Relation to the Picturesque', and it is tempting to see some of these images as reflecting these ideas. For Frith the very land must have had significance, as this was the land on which the stories of the Bible were played out. However, in writing about the Sinaitic script he does not lose a certain scientific objectivity – he rejects the view that the script was 'Israelitish'. The Sinai peninsular was the site of turquoise mines during the time of the ancient Egyptians, and became associated with the goddess Hathor, whose temple is at Serabit el-Khadim. No sign of this is found in the images here, however.

Mount Horeb (534, page 180) would certainly have been viewed by Frith as the mountain of God: here God manifested himself to Moses and delivered the Ten Commandments. The convent (536, page 182) is a monastery built on the orders of Justinian between 527 and 565 on the supposed site of the burning bush. It is the oldest working monastery in the world. Frith's photograph shows a very unusual view of it. The convent is normally shown from the opposite side, with the emphasis on the building, but Frith's view emphasises the isolation of the place. It highlights a jumble of boulders, with the fort-like buildings of the convent peeping above a dip in the landscape. His commentary on this image also seems to stress the isolation of the subject: the convent was '... the first sight of a human abode in the vast and desolate solitude', and later in the same passage he writes: 'The scene is strangely desolate'. These descriptions fit Frith's ideas about the monastery standing as a kind of fortress for Christianity in a sea of Islam. Thus image and commentary work together to create the emotional impact that was intended.

Justinian, from a Mosaic

This desolation is also seen in the photograph of Gebel Moosa (527E, page 178), in which we can see one of Frith's tents somewhat precariously perched on the side of an incline (from other photographs we can detect that he seems to have travelled with three tents, one of which was black and served as his mobile darkroom). This photograph highlights the physical difficulty of photography in these conditions.

MOUNT SERBAL, *From the Wadee Feyran c1860* 532

The desolate spot (532, opposite) shows a view of Mount Serbal on the Sinai peninsula, one of the possible candidates for the mountain where Moses received the Ten Commandments. It is one of the highest in the Sinai at 6,690 feet. The precise location of Mount Sinai is a matter of hot dispute, although the inscriptions found near Mount Serbal have led many, including the Egyptologists Lepsius and Ebers, to believe that it is indeed the location of this important Biblical site. It was sketched by Roberts, and later photographed by a one-time assistant of Frith, Frank Mason Good, whose trips to the Middle East were financed by Frith, and whose photographs were published in collections of stereoscopic prints.

The Dead Sea (right) is the lowest surface of water anywhere in the world, lying 1,312 ft below sea level. It was visited by Frith on his 1858 trip to the Holy Land. Its strangeness and bleakness seems to have been a magnet for artists of the time. Indeed, this photograph reminds us of Holman Hunt's painting 'The Scapegoat' (1854), which was painted here. Holman Hunt visited the Dead Sea in October and November 1854 as part of his tour of the Holy Land, believing it to be site of Sodom and Gomorrah. Just as the overt purpose of 'The Scapegoat' was to embody Biblical history, it seems certain that this was also the purpose of Frith's photograph. The theory that it was Biblical associations that inspired him tends to be supported by the fact that Frith provided photographs for an 1862 version of the Bible – the Queen's Bible.

THE DEAD SEA, *Rocks Covered with Salt c2000*
BY KIND PERMISSION OF TODD BOLEN/BIBLEPLACES.COM

'Its buoyancy is proverbial. It is probable that, from its extreme saltness, neither animal nor vegetable life can exist in it; but it is beautifully bright, and had no offensive smell. I saw gazelles almost upon its shores, and the footprints of a very large hyena close to the water's edge.'

Frith's Notes to Photograph 590E *(opposite)*

Perhaps there is not a spot upon earth which is popularly invested with more ill-defined and mysterious interest than the Dead Sea; and although a practical acquaintance with its peculiarities may dispel some of the unsubstantial images which are supposed to haunt its shores, or float over its surface, there will yet remain enough of strangeness, and loneliness, and unaccountability, to entitle it to class as one of the most remarkable natural objects upon the face of the globe.

I believe that many persons are under the impression that this sea did not exist previous to the overthrow of the 'cities of the plain'. This, however, is not the case; for although it is not mentioned at all in the New Testament, we find it alluded to as early as Gen. xiv. 3, where it is called 'The Salt Sea'; and again in Deut. iv. 49. 'The Sea of the Plain', or the 'Arabah'; and in Joel ii. 20, 'The Eastern Sea'. It is now called by the Arabs 'The Bahr-el-Lut', or the 'Sea of Lot'. It is probable that at the time of the destruction of Sodom, this sea overflowed its southern boundaries, overwhelming a beautiful and well-watered plain, upon which stood the five doomed cities. In the year 1848, Lieutenant Lynch, an officer in the United States service, sailed over this sea in all directions, and made many interesting observations. He found the greatest depth to be 1308 feet, and its depression below the level of the Mediterranean 1316 feet – I believe, without doubt, the lowest part of the surface of our globe. Many conjectures have been hazarded to account for this extraordinary depression; the fact, however, accounts for several of the phenomena which distinguish the Dead Sea, such as the great heat and consequent evaporation from its surface, sufficient, it would appear, to carry off the large flood of water which the River Jordan, and other streams in the south, constantly pour into it; – for the sea has now no outlet. When I was there, in the month of May, the thermometer rose to 130 degrees Fahr.

The various salts constitute rather more than one-fourth of the entire specific gravity of the water. Its buoyancy is proverbial. It is probable that, from its extreme saltness, neither animal nor vegetable life can exist in it; but it is beautifully bright, and had no offensive smell. I saw gazelles almost upon its shores, and the footprints of a very large hyena close to the water's edge.

The Dead Sea, *The North Shore 1858* 590E

AQABAAH, *An Encampment under Shittim Trees, Wady c1861* 540

Here we see two of Frith's tents resting in a grove of trees on the floor of a valley or wadi. The shittim is what we would today call a variety of acacia, the acacia seyal; the Biblical name is derived from the Hebrew word 'shittah', meaning 'thorny'. This is perhaps an unremarkable image, but to Frith, and no doubt to his readers, the words shittim wood and Wady El Ithm had religious resonance. The Tabernacle was made of shittim wood, and possibly the Ark of the Covenant was made of it as well. The wadi is probably the route that the Israelites took after they were refused entry to Edom on their journey to the Promised Land. We can imagine Frith's state of mind as he rested in the solitude of the desert, following in the footsteps of Moses through the wilderness.

JERUSALEM, *Between Jerusalem and Jericho c1861* 562

JERUSALEM, *The Pool of Hezekiah c1857* 572

The Photographs – JERUSALEM

The first selection of Frith's photographs contained a portrait of Francis Frith, and photographs of the Sphinx, the temple at Koum Ombos, and the Pool of Hezekiah in Jerusalem (572, page 189). They were taken during Frith's first excursions in Egypt and the Holy Land, and were accompanied by his own text. Clearly the marketing mind of the photographer, or at least his publishers, was operating with this selection, which showed a familiar image of ancient Egypt, a rather more obscure image of the same country, and an image to tempt the many clergymen who were subscribers to the project.

Jerusalem is a site of archaeological, historical, and religious significance. The history of the city reflects the importance that it has for Christianity, Islam and Judaism, and the monuments recorded by Frith show a complex relationship to one another, and to the history of the site.

Photograph 572 (page 189) looks out over the Pool of Hezekiah to the Church of the Holy Sepulchre, and must have been taken from what was the Citadel, which was built in 1310–11. It looks out over the Christian quarter of the city, with the pool in the foreground, which is also known as the Pool of the Patriarch or the Towers Pool. The pools were established to provide the vast amount of water used in the temple.

This was the first of Frith's photographs of the Holy Land to be reproduced, so the text that Frith wrote to accompany the image is of particular interest. He is singularly unimpressed with the local population, but he is captivated by the thought of being in such a holy location, although the dilapidation of the church seems to depress him. In this he shows the familiar attitudes of the mid-Victorian traveller to the Middle East.

FRITH'S NOTES TO PHOTOGRAPH 572 *(page 189)*

I do not envy the man who can enter unmoved the land –

'Where the holiest of memories, phantom-like, throng.'

If he has no organ of veneration, he had better stop at home and read 'Eothen.' I cannot write lightly of Holy Palestine. It is true that the natural features of the country are, for the most part, monotonous and comparatively uninteresting – that the towns are paltry and dirty in the extreme – that the Turkish Mohammedan population is ignorant and bigoted – that the Arabs who infest its solitudes are the laziest, the most cowardly, and worthless set of fellows – in a word, and in every use of it, the greatest vagabonds in existence; yet in spite of it, and overwhelming it all triumphantly, comes the thrilling recollection that this was the country of Abraham and the Prophets! these the cities of David! and - first and last, and mingling with every line of its eventful history - that this was the spot of his earth chosen by its Creator from the beginning, upon which the plan of his salvation should be finished. It was in Palestine that he was made flesh and dwelt among men. And it was especially in Jerusalem and its neighbourhood that he fulfilled his ministry, manifested his Divine nature, and finally, in one awful hour, 'in his own body on the tree,' sustained the accumulated sins, and suffered the concentrated agony of the whole human race. No wonder that men have striven to perpetuate the local memories of even the most trivial events of this glorious and awful period. And yet,

'It is true that the natural features of the country are, for the most part, monotonous and comparatively uninteresting – that the towns are paltry and dirty in the extreme – that the Turkish Mohammedan population is ignorant and bigoted – that the Arabs who infest its solitudes are the laziest ... yet, in spite of all this, and overwhelming it all triumphantly, comes the thrilling recollection – that this was the country of Abraham and the Prophets!'

in spite of man's most earnest endeavours, most of these localities are irretrievably lost: even the site of the Holy Sepulchre is doubtful. May we not recognize in this uncertainty - to which we find a parallel in the concealment of the burial-place of Moses - the hand of Providence defeating the tendency of mankind to place-worship, and its attendant ceremonials?

I shall have more to say respecting the general features of modern Jerusalem, in connection with some other of my views: I confine myself, at present, to a short notice of the more prominent objects in the picture before us, viz., the Pool of Hezekiah, and the Church of the Holy Sepulchre. We read (2 Kings xx. 20), that 'Hezekiah made a pool and a conduit, and brought water into the city'; and also (2 Chron. xxxii. 30), that he 'stopped the upper water-course of Gihon, and brought it straight down to the west side of the city of David'. Upon this Dr. Robinson observes: – 'From this language we can only infer that Hezekiah constructed a pool within the city on its western part. To such a pool the present reservoir, which is doubtless an ancient work, entirely corresponds; and it is also fed in a similar manner.' The buildings with railings extending over the Pool are 'The Mediterranean', and other hotels, and will probably be familiar to many of my readers. The Pool still continues to supply the city with water. It is 240 feet long, by 144 feet broad.

The dilapidated domes of the Church of the Holy Sepulchre proclaim its present condition; but the front is a good specimen of Byzantine architecture. It is in the joint possession of the Greek and Latin churches, and the ceremonies performed in it at Easter have been described by a host of travellers. It was formerly, and more appropriately, called the Church of the Resurrection. It has been twice, at least, totally destroyed: once in the seventh, and again in the eleventh century; and as late as 1808, the greater part of the church and the whole of the cupola were destroyed by fire. The identity of the site, as before remarked, is very questionable: we are told that the Sepulchre was in 'a garden nigh at hand', where Jesus was crucified; and the crucifixion took place without the walls. Dr. Robinson satisfied himself by a survey from the very spot on which tins view Avas taken, that the present site could never have been excluded by the second wall (see his 'Researches', vol. i. p. 410).

JERUSALEM, *From the Mount of Olives 1859* 566

JERUSALEM FROM THE MOUNT OF OLIVES.

WE have already given a distant view of Jerusalem from Mount Scopus. Our present picture is taken much nearer the City; from a point on the Mount of Olives, about half way up, and directly opposite the Golden Gate (now closed). In the foreground are some venerable olive trees. It is very difficult to assign their age, but the vitality of the olive is known to be very great. In the Garden of Gethsemane, which lies in the bottom of the valley, covered by the foreground of the present view, are a few trees of still greater antiquity. The Dome of the Mosque of Omar again appears conspicuously. Beneath the area wall, where it terminates abruptly on the right, is held to have been situated the Pool of Bethesda. A little to the right of the dome is the Church of the Holy Sepulchre; and to the left of it, nearly on the horizon, is the tower of the Citadel—the "Tower of Hippicus"—from which our bird's-eye view of the City and of the Pool of Hezekiah were taken. Under the City wall, on this side, may be seen the stones of the Mohammedan Cemetery. Beneath them, chiefly on this side the valley, are innumerable records of Jewish burial—this being the Valley of Jehoshaphat, where every Hebrew would fain have his ashes to rest. Thousands of aged Jews resort to Jerusalem solely that their bones may lie here.

In other articles which accompany the various views in and around Jerusalem, we have given a concise history of its many vicissitudes, as well as occasional notices of its present condition. Let us now glance at the most important remains of antiquity which are still to be found. It cannot be expected that after nineteen sieges, and several complete demolitions, there are many very conspicuous objects of antiquarian interest in Jerusalem. But the Christian traveller has still the delightful satisfaction of recognizing, beyond doubt, many of the *sites* of events. The natural features of the country are bold and well-defined. Here the Great Temple of the Old Dispensation stood—yonder is Mount Zion; below lie the valleys of Hinnom and Jehoshaphat; and opposite rises the Mount of Olives, with its many sweet and sacred associations, and its fine prospect, on the one hand, of the city and neighbourhood, and on the other of the mountainous country towards Jericho, with the deep blue waters of the Dead Sea in their hot recess, and the silver-line of the Jordan, as it flows down from the Sea of Galilee. Here, surely, are subjects for days of contemplation and enjoyment. You would never tire of sitting under the shade of one of these old olive trees in the month of April, dreamily inhaling the very atmosphere of sacred history. But to return to the antiquities:—Perhaps the only remains of very ancient Jewish masonry are the stones in the south-east corner of the city wall, some of which are of great size—24 feet long, 6 feet broad, and 3 feet high—and which, as Dr. Robinson observes, "at once strike the eye of the beholder as ancient; as being, at least, as old as the time of Herod, if not of Solomon." Also, the remains of an arch in the outer wall of the Mosque of Aksa, which probably formed the starting-point of a bridge over the Tyropean valley, connecting Mounts Moriah and Zion; and lastly the lower courses of the Great Wall, now called the "Wall of Wailing," where the modern Jews purchase the right of approaching the site of their temple, of wailing over its downfall, and praying for the restoration of "Israel."

'... Opposite rises the Mount of Olives, with its many sweet and sacred associations ... here, surely are subjects for days of contemplation and enjoyment. You would never tire of sitting under the shade of one of these old olive trees in the month of April, dreamily inhaling the very atmosphere of sacred history.'

FACSIMILE REPRODUCTION OF FRITH'S NOTES TO PHOTOGRAPH 566 (OPPOSITE)

JERUSALEM, *The Dome of the Rock, from the Lutheran Tower c2000*
BY KIND PERMISSION OF TODD BOLEN/BIBLEPLACES.COM

Photograph 566 (page 192) was taken on a later expedition in the Holy Land in 1859, and was published in the second selection with a commentary by the Pooles. It shows a general view of Jerusalem looking west from the Mount of Olives towards the Dome of the Rock. This building, holy to Muslims, Jews and Christians, was erected by Caliph Abd el-Malik, one of the Umayyad caliphs, in AD 641. Its purpose was to guard the Foundation Stone from which Mohammed ascended to heaven, and it is regarded by both Jews and some Christians as a manifestation of Solomon's temple; it thus became a church in Crusader times.

FRITH'S NOTES TO PHOTOGRAPH 573E *(opposite)*

The view is taken from the western slope of the mount, at some distance above the valley. Before us is a small Arab village around the Church of the Ascension, founded by the Empress Helena. After what we have said as to the holy sites generally, and especially that of the Sepulchre, the reader will not be disposed to lay great stress upon the selection of this place by the pious empress. Probably it was chosen from its striking position, but this would be a very poor reason for its identity, and rather, we think, weigh against it. The building itself does not require a particular description.

By turning through 180 degrees from the vantage point of picture 566, Frith would have been able to see this view of the Church of the Ascension on the Mount of Olives (573E, opposite). In the foreground we see examples of the trees which give the hill its name. The church was founded by Helena, the mother of Constantine. It was then renovated by Modestos, head of the Theodosius Monastery, and the Bishop of Alexandria, John the Pious, in the brief period of Persian rule (614-638). Surrounding it we can see an Arab village.

JERUSALEM, *The Church of the Ascension c1857* 573E

JERUSALEM, *From Mount Scopus c1857* 567 (DETAIL)

This view is taken almost exactly due north of the location of picture 573E (page 195), but it was probably the first of the two to be taken. It looks south-west back over Jerusalem, and shows the extent of the city at this time. The walls and the Dome of the Rock are visible in the middle distance towards the top of the frame. When this picture (and most of Frith's photographs) of Jerusalem was taken, a period of rapid expansion outside the city walls was just beginning; thus they record a phase of the city that was to very rapidly disappear.

In this view Frith was either consciously or unconsciously echoing views of the same place by James Graham and Thomas Seddon. Seddon painted a large view of the valley of Jehoshaphat which was exhibited in London in March 1855, as well as a view of the well itself. James Graham took many photographs of the same place. We can see the city of Jerusalem in the distance on the top of the hill, with the Dome of the Rock dominating the scene.

JERUSALEM, *From the Well of En-Rogel c1857* 568 (DETAIL)

JERUSALEM, *Tombs in the Valley of Jehoshaphat c1857* 574

Photograph 574 (previous page) shows tombs in the Valley of Kidron, although Frith referred to it as the Valley of Jehoshaphat. This lay beneath the temple walls, which would have been to the left of the frame, and was considered a most prestigious burial place. We see three tombs in the view. From the right they are the tomb of Zechariah, the tomb of the Hezirs, and the Pillar of Absalom. Only one tomb, the tomb of the Hezirs, records the real names of the people buried there; the Hezirs were a wealthy priestly family from the first century AD. The pillar of Absalom was carved from the rock face in the time of Herod, and was later used as a dwelling by Byzantine monks. A clearer image of this tomb can be seen in photograph 578E, opposite. The tomb of Zechariah also dates form the first century AD, but it is not known for whom it was intended, nor whether it was in fact completed.

JERUSALEM, *The Mount of Olives and the Pillar of Absalom c2000*
BY KIND PERMISSION OF TODD BOLEN/BIBLEPLACES.COM

FRITH'S NOTES TO PHOTOGRAPH 578E *(opposite)*

It is very remarkable that the arts and monuments of sepulchre should be amongst the most interesting and important relics of the nations of antiquity.

With reference to Egypt, where the custom of embalmment obtained, and the tombs were decorated with paintings and sculpture, the antiquarian student possesses no richer source of interest and information; and very frequently in Palestine the first objects which arrest the attention of the traveller are the sepulchral excavations, which mark the sites of lost cities, and in many cases are almost their only records. Many of my photographic pictures were made in TOMBS! To save myself the trouble of pitching my dark tent, and also for the sake of their greater coolness, I very often availed myself of a rock-tomb. Around Jerusalem there are many excavated sepulchres – as those called the Tombs of the Judges and Kings, and great numbers on the southern and eastern slopes of the Valley of Hinnum, where the Aceldama, or 'field of blood', is shown, a site which has obtained credit from at least the time of Jerome. The Tomb of Absalom, of which we now give a

JERUSALEM, *Absalom's Tomb c1857* 578E

representation, is situated in the Valley of Jehoshaphat, close to the lower bridge over the Kedron. The lower portion is a square block, cut from the adjoining rock, having a niche left around it. It is 24 feet square, and has on each side columns of the Ionic order, with pilasters at the corners. This portion of the structure is about 20 feet high; the upper portion consists of masonry of large stones. There are first two flat layers, and above these 'a small dome or cupola runs up into a low spire, which spreads a little at the top, like an opening flower.' This masonry is about 20 feet high, giving to the whole an elevation of about 40 feet. There is a small excavated chamber in the body of the tomb, into which, says Dr Robinson, a hole had already been broken through one of the sides, several centuries ago.

It may disappoint some of our readers, if we inform them that there is very small probability that this tomb has any connexion whatever with the man to whom tradition has allotted it. The fact is, that this structure, as well as the neighbouring ones, called the Tombs of Jehoshaphat and Zachariah, have all the character of Roman works. Absalom, at any rate, can scarcely be held to have been buried here; for he was cast into a pit at Beersheba, near to the place where he was slain, and a heap of stones was raised over his body as a token of infamy. There is no probability that the kingly column raised by Absalom himself in the King's Dale (2 Sam. xviii. 18) to his own honour was intended for a sepulchral monument. We do not read that he was buried there; and the present structure has nothing of the character of the architecture of that time.

JERUSALEM, *The Pool of Bethesda c1857* 576E

It was here (576E, opposite) that Jesus healed the cripple in John chapter 5. The pool lies amongst the tumble of apparent ruins towards the bottom of the picture. Modern excavations have shown the depth of the pool, which would have been used as a water store rather than as a bathing or washing place. Behind the tumble rises the Dome of the Rock.

Frith's Notes to Photograph 577 *(page 203)*

In the valley of the Brook Kidron, on the steep side facing the south-eastern extremity of Jerusalem, stands the picturesque Arab village of Siloam. The inhabitants live partly in houses, and partly in excavations in the rock, which are probably ancient tombs. In the view we look towards the south. Immediately beneath is the bed of the Kidron, with tombs beyond it, on the further bank. Above this slope the rock rises steeply, and the village, like so many in Palestine, is perched like a cluster of nests upon the rough cliff. The square houses, with their small windows, look like so many little forts. Above and beneath the village are a few trees. To the right, in the valley below, is a pretty patch of wood, and beyond all rises the Hill of Evil Counsel. In the valley are three fountains, the most famous of which is that called the Pool of Siloam. There is no reason to doubt its being that mentioned as the Pool of Siloam in the Old Testament (Neh. iii. 15), and as the Pool of Siloam in the New (John ix. 11), in the account of the healing of the blind man by Our Lord. The Prophet Isaiah is supposed to refer to the same fountain: 'Forasmuch as this people refuseth the waters of Shiloah that go softly, and rejoice in Rezin and Remaliah's son; now therefore, behold, the Lord bringeth up upon them the waters of the river, strong and many, [even] the king of Assyria, and all his glory: and he shall come up over all his channels, and go over all his banks.' (Isaiah viii. 6, 7.) Here the reference seems to be to a running stream of some importance, and Kidron may, therefore, be meant, instead of the fountain, or the stream flowing from it. The mention of the king of Syria may convey an allusion to the famous streams of his capital, of which Naaman said, in his pride, '[Are] not Abana and Pharpar, rivers of Damascus, better than all the waters of Israel?' (2 Kings v. 12.)

The Pool of Siloam is without the view, to the right; for it is beyond the main valley, just within the Tyropœon, a position mentioned by Josephus. The water flows out of an artificial basin under the cliff into a large reservoir, fifty-three feet long, eighteen feet wide, and nineteen feet deep. It is faced with stone, and steps lead down to the bottom. The water passes out by a channel, which is at first covered, but afterwards becomes an open stream which waters several gardens beneath. The basin is not the natural exit of the fountain, but the end of a subterranean passage, 1750 feet long, from the Fountain of the Virgin, which is situate on the west side of the main valley opposite the north extremity of the village of

Siloam. Both fountains have a singular ebb and flow: their water is pleasant to the taste. The Pool of Siloam, like most of those which are within and around Jerusalem, is an extremely picturesque object. Its ruined masonry, overgrown with clinging vegetation, gives it a look of patriarchal antiquity, and the women who come down with their water-jars complete the picture, which would be true of the place at any time past for three thousand years or more, so unchanged is Eastern life.

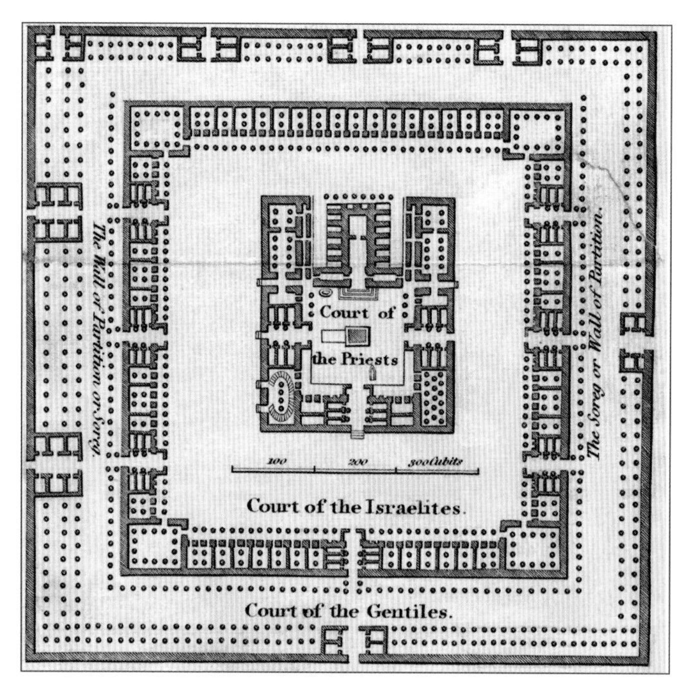

Plan of the The Temple of Jerusalem
A fanciful 18th-century plan based on little archaeological evidence

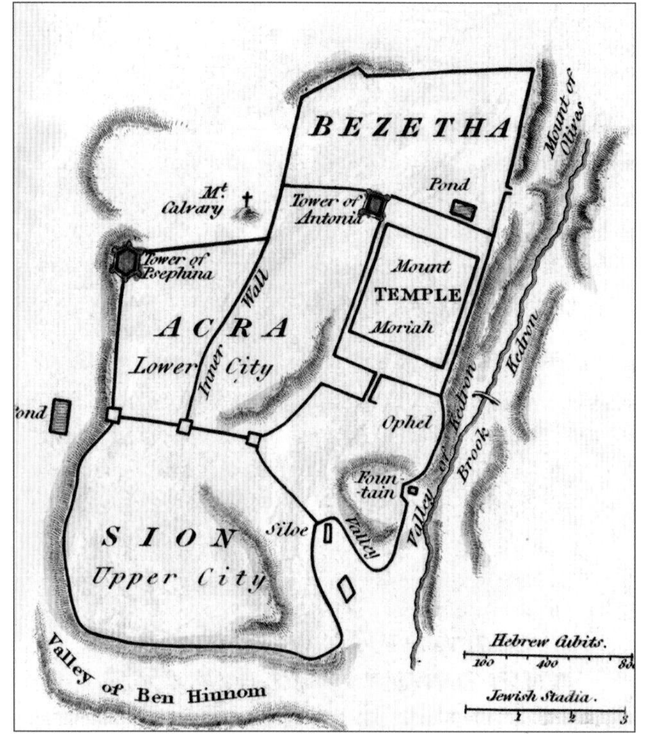

Plan of Jerusalem c1750

The Kidron Valley (577, opposite) leads into the Valley of Jehoshaphat. The village of Siloam is the site of one of the pools of Jerusalem, the source of a natural spring, which was the reputed site of the healing of the blind man in the New Testament. It lies almost due south of the Temple Mount, which is out of view in this image. The valley winds around to the north and the top of the frame below the walls of the city.

JERUSALEM, *The Village of Siloam and the Valley of Kidron c1857* 577

JERUSALEM, *The Entrance to the Church of the Holy Sepulchre c1857* 580

The church of the Holy Sepulchre was built in the time of the Emperor Constantine on the site of a Roman temple to Aphrodite. The architect was Zenubius, a Syrian; the church was consecrated in 355. The holiest part, under a large gold dome (visible in photograph 581E, page 206), is the tomb of Christ. Whether the tomb is actually that of Christ is debated in the commentary to the picture. The Pooles' comment upon the somewhat dilapidated appearance of the church; this was because it had been damaged by fire in 1808. It caused Frith much consternation to see the sad state of such a significant religious site.

FRITH'S NOTES TO PHOTOGRAPH 580

This view represents the entrance and principal front of the Church of the Holy Sepulchre. In examining it we are first struck by a singular incongruity, very faithfully preserved by photography. The style of the architecture, and the decay of much of the more delicate work, gives the building an air of age that is in contrast with the fresh aspect of a great part of the masonry which, moreover, supports or is connected with the apparently older work. This is explained by the history of the church. In the year 1808 it was destroyed by fire, and rebuilt by the Greeks, who faithfully followed its old form, using, wherever it was possible, the former materials. It was fortunate that they did so, for not only have they no ecclesiastical style of their own, but they have thus preserved in the exterior a most interesting record of the Crusaders. Their work

JERUSALEM, *The Church of the Holy Sepulchre, from the Lutheran Tower c2000*
BY KIND PERMISSION OF TODD BOLEN/BIBLEPLACES.COM

would, indeed, in its faithfulness, put to shame many European restorations. It affords an instance of the extreme care with which the Eastern churches keep to ancient forms. In like manner the carvings which are made by the monks of Palestine for sale to pilgrims are exactly what would have been made by their predecessors a thousand years ago. Certainly they have not advanced with the times. An observer unused to the East will be astonished at the neglect which is apparent in a building held in higher reverence

'An observer unused to the East will be astonished at the neglect which is apparent in a building held in higher reverence than any other by the Eastern Christians.'

than any other by the Eastern Christians, and not very long since restored at great cost. There is not only an air of general dilapidation, but on a ledge beneath one of the windows is an unsightly crowd of jars and the like, protected by a rude rail, while a ladder, attached to the wall, forms a means of descending to the ledge. The mosques and churches, except those of the Armenians, and some of the Greeks, almost invariably show the utmost neglect, beautiful portions being walled up, as is the case with the doorway to the right in the present instance, and fragile ornamental details, which a little care would save, being suffered to go to ruin.

The exterior of the Church of the Holy Sepulchre, as seen in this view, although it suffers much from the mean style of the upper portion, presents a very picturesque appearance. The Norman doorways, with their rich clustered columns and well-proportioned arches, showing a fine mixture of bold and delicate work, and the not less beautiful, but much injured, windows above, one of which has been partly blocked up, are worthy memorials of the Crusaders. Although not on a grand scale, nor displaying the breadth that renders many of our Norman churches admirable, this front is in a style at once pure and rich.

JERUSALEM, *A Street View with the Church of the Holy Sepulchre 1857* 581E

FRITH'S NOTES TO PHOTOGRAPH 581E *(opposite)*

The ruined state of modern Jerusalem is strikingly brought before us by this view. The Church of the Holy Sepulchre has outside the aspect of a place long deserted, so that we could not imagine, did we know, that it is still the object of pilgrimages, and in the hands of rich Christian communities. The great square tower is seen to have partly fallen, the smaller, but loftier, towers to be decayed, and the chief dome to have lost half its outer covering. This last has lately been restored, but so long as the rain does not penetrate into the interior, the external appearance of the church is wholly neglected. The houses nearer to us seem uninhabited, so miserable is their state. The street to the left, with its pavement sloping to the middle, and the ragged awnings of the shops, is harmonious in its wretchedness. Everything looks as though the city had been sacked, and was now almost or entirely uninhabited. The Norman church, rising from the oriental houses in striking contrast, recalls at once the time of the Crusaders, whose monuments, records of their inflexible national feeling, show nothing borrowed from the land of their sojourning.

ABOVE: JERUSALEM, *The City Wall and the Mosque of Omar c1857* 575E

Frith's commentary on photograph 575E (above) places his photograph next to the city walls by the Temple Mount; the dip in the landscape before us is called the Tyropoeon Valley. Frith calls the dome in the middle distance the Mosque of Omar, another name for the Dome of the Rock. There is another Mosque of Omar sited in the eastern part of the church of the Holy Sepulchre; it commemorated the place where Caliph Omar prayed, having captured the city. This was burnt down in 938. In Crusader times this tradition was forgotten, and the existing Mosque of Omar was built to the south of the church. The Dome of the Rock is the mosque built over the site from which Mohammed is reputed to have ascended to heaven. Frith's view is clearly of the latter. Wenham, who was Frith's assistant, records difficulties in getting close to the mosque to take a photograph, as local Muslim fanatics were attacking them.

'A vast number of the Mohammedan inhabitants sought refuge within the sacred enclosure; the "Christians," however, broke in upon them, and committed the most terrible atrocities – neither age nor sex were spared.'

Frith's Notes to Photograph 575E *(previous page)*

The present walls of Jerusalem, which were built by the Saracens about 700 years ago – although excluding large spaces which were comprehended in the ancient city – are still a 'world too wide' for its shrunk dimensions: accordingly we find a considerable space of waste ground within, and running almost the whole round of these walls. Here (in my picture) is a piece of it, with a few bushes of prickly pear, on the left of the picture. On the other side is a portion of the interior of the city wall. The accumulation of rubbish is so great on this inner side that the outer wall is fully 20 feet deeper: indeed, it is pretty clear that the general level of the original Jewish city must be on an average of at least 20 feet below the present surface. The space which intervenes between the foreground of this picture and the mosque is the Tyropean Valley, over which was a bridge connecting the Mounts Moriah and Zion.

Some large stones, representing the spring of an arch, which are found in the outer wall of the temple area, are conjectured to mark the commencement of this bridge. They were first brought into notice by Dr. Robinson, and constitute one of the very few remnants of early Jewish masonry now existing in Jerusalem. The entire temple area, upon which now stand the mosques of Omar and Aksa, besides other buildings, is called by the Moslems, El Haram-esh-Sherif, or the 'Holy Sanctuary.' The great mosque they call Kubbet-es-Lukkrah, 'Dome of the Rock.' It is a handsome octagonal building, standing on a platform near the centre of the area, from which it is elevated by several steps.

It was in A.D. 636 that the Caliph Omar, the reputed founder of this mosque, took possession of the Holy City; but it is also related that it was rebuilt by the Caliph Abd-el-Melek, in the year 686. In 1099, when the Crusaders, under Godfrey of Bouillon, took Jerusalem, a vast number of the Mohammedan inhabitants sought refuge within the sacred enclosure; the "Christians," however, broke in upon them, and committed the most terrible atrocities – neither age nor sex were spared. According to Christian writers more than 10,000 (the Arab authors say 70,000) were slain around this mosque, and 'the whole area was covered ankle deep with blood.' Then the "Christians" made haste to consecrate this place to its original worship; but, in 1187, the Moslems again, under Saladin, recovered the city, and purified the sacred precincts with rose-water from Damascus, and from that day they have not ceased to cherish and venerate it as the most sacred spot of earth, after the Kabeh of Mecca ...

Jerusalem was conquered by Caliph Omar Ibn el-Khattab in 638, and Arab rule then lasted until 1099. The Aqsa Mosque (585, previous page) was built between 705 and 715, and may mark the end of Mohammed's ride to Jerusalem – 'aqsa' is the Arabic for 'end'. Jerusalem is of great importance to Muslims: it is the Holy City of David and the prophets, as well as being the site of Mohammed's ascent into heaven. During this period of Arab rule, therefore, the city prospered as tribute in the form of taxes flowed in.

JERUSALEM, *Al Aqsa Mosque, from the Lutheran Tower c2000*
BY KIND PERMISSION OF TODD BOLEN/BIBLEPLACES.COM

FRITH'S NOTES TO PHOTOGRAPH 585 *(previous page)*

The traveller may seek for this view by entering the city at the Zion Gate, turning sharp round to the right, and proceeding close by the wall, in the direction of the Temple area. He will probably pass on the outskirts of the Jew's quarter a number of leprous persons of both sexes, who crouch up by the way-side – clamorously soliciting alms from the passer. These wretched people, whose appearance is exceedingly repulsive, and who subsist entirely upon charity, are yet said to intermarry aamongst their own class! In this outskirt of the city, moreover, not only the eye is offended, but all the senses suffer severely. Run through it, I entreat you, until you reach a deserted tract, and some cultivated land. Yes! – a ploughed field within the walls of Jerusalem! Ascend the wall at the corner of this field, and you will obtain the view which I now give. You will see by the depth of that outer wall, what ruin, what debris of former grandeur has accumulated within the walls. There is evidently at this point, some twenty-five feet of rubbish over the original level of the soil; and this is probably not much more than the average deposit which is now spread over the whole city.

In sinking the foundations of the new Protestant Episcopal Church, which are based upon the solid rock, many feet of rubbish had to be removed, and some curious remains of ancient construction were discovered. Amongst the rubbish accumulated on other parts of Mount Zion, small, quadrangular bricks, of a light colour – the remains of tesselated pavement – are very abundant.

The Austrian Hospice, now in the course of erection, will be a large and substantial building: it is probable that nothing equal to it has been produced within the walls since the time of the Crusaders. Its foundations required deep and extensive excavations, but it does not appear that many objects of interest were brought to light. To procure the stone for this building, a very fair road, about a league in length, has been made to some ancient quarries, which had been re-opened for this purpose. The waggons – the only wheeled carriages which we saw in use at Jerusalem – are the same which had formerly been employed for the Balaklava railway.

Whatever difference of opinion there may be as to the expediency of having a society expressly constituted for the conversion of Jews, there can be no doubt that a beneficial influence is exerted by the presence of the good men and women connected with it, and more especially by the hospital which it maintains, under the able management of Dr. Macgown and E. Atkinson, Esq. Notwithstanding the shyness which difference of religious opinion is too apt to create, an amicable co-operation has, in many instances, been the happy result, and these excellent medical officers are on friendly terms with their Israelite brethren. The Christian schools connected with the mission, as well as the schools for girls established and maintained by the liberality of Sir Moses Montefiore, and all that supported by finds bequeathed by a wealthy German for Israelite boys, are also productive of manifest advantages, not merely to Jerusalem, but to the neighbouring country.

JERUSALEM, *The Golden Gate c2000*
BY KIND PERMISSION OF TODD BOLEN/BIBLEPLACES.COM

For Christians this gate (587, overleaf) is the Golden Gate, one of the gates of the temple called the Beautiful Gate, through which Jesus entered the temple to cleanse it, and near which St Peter healed a cripple. For the Jews it is the Shushan Gate, and many prayed here before the building of a Muslim cemetery made them pray at the Western Wall. For the Muslims this gate is the Gate of Mercy mentioned in one of the shuras of the Koran. There is some debate about the precise date of the present structure; it dates perhaps from the Byzantine period, or perhaps from the Arab Umayyad period (661–750).

JERUSALEM, *The Golden Gate c1861* 587

MAR SABA, *The Convent c1857* 579E

The monastery of Mar Saba (579E, above) is evidence of the monasticism of the early church in the Middle East. In the 4th century, many Christian monks escaped into the Judean desert to escape the secular world. Among these was St Sabas (439–532), who founded this monastery in the Kidron Valley about six miles south-east of Jerusalem. The foundation was a 'laura', or a community of monks living individual hermit-like lives. In this it differed from a community who all live by one rule. From the 8th to the 9th century the monastery was an important spiritual centre, and it gained the protection of Charlemagne. It was here that John of Damascus was ordained a priest.

FRITH'S NOTES TO PHOTOGRAPH 579E

When the traveller has satisfied the first cravings of curiosity, or has somewhat appeased the fever of interest in which he entered the holy city, he usually projects an excursion to Jericho and the Dead Sea, via the Convent of Santa Sarba: so, under the conduct of two or three of the Jericho Arabs (who, when not the guards, have from time immemorial been the thieves of this road of good-Samaritan fame), he ambles down the valley of the Kedron, past the well of Enrogel, and after a ride of some four hours, encamps at the entrance of the rocky defile which the winter torrent has worn for itself in its course to the Dead Sea, and upon the southern slope of which, a mile or two further down, the convent is built; or he proceeds at once to the convent, and claims the hospitality of its inmates for the night.

The magnificently wild and deep ravine forms a sternly appropriate clinging-place for this old ascetic pile. We dont pretend to have done anything like justice to the subject in our photograph. The view should be taken from the other side of the ravine, from which the whole of the building and the entire depth of the ravine could perhaps be rendered. So 'impossible' are its sides, that to have reached this point would have involved another day's labour. Amongst the rocks surrounding the convent we killed three or four brace of partridges.

NAZARETH, *From the North West c1857* 594E

NAZARETH, *An Aerial View from the North-east c2000*

BY KIND PERMISSION OF TODD BOLEN/BIBLEPLACES.COM

The history and importance of Nazareth (549E, opposite) needs little introduction. Frith in his notes uses quotations from a number of sources, almost as if his powers of description have let him down at this site. The picture shows a small village nestling on a hillside with the minaret of a mosque in the centre. Nazareth is the place from which Mary and Joseph set out for the census that took them to Bethlehem.

It was in Nazareth that Jesus probably grew up. It is today the largest Arab town in Israel.

BAALBEC, *The Great Pillars and the Smaller Temple c1857* 613

BAALBEC, *From the South c1857* 610E

BAALBEC.

GENERAL VIEW FROM THE SOUTH.

IN order to enable our readers to judge of the points from which our views of Baalbec have been taken, we have engraved a plan of the ancient city and of the temples, compiled principally after the careful surveys of Wood and Dawkins. It has been conjectured that the entire plan of the temples of Baalbec was not carried out; and that it was contemplated to erect another building on the northern side of the Great Temple, corresponding with the smaller structure.

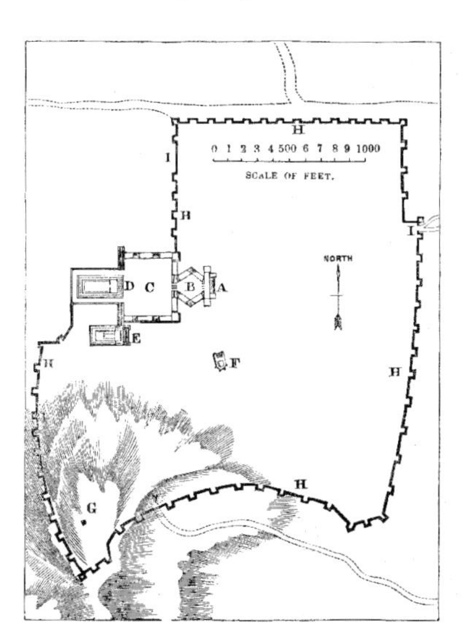

A. The Flight of Steps, and the Portico, which is 260 feet long. It had 12 columns, which were, with the pedestals, 57 feet high.

B. Hexagonal Court, or Forum, 190 feet long, by 266 wide.

C. Quadrangular Court, 405 feet long, by 440 wide.

D. Great Temple, 290 feet long, by 160 wide. (The six columns shown in the view belonged to this temple.)

E. The smaller Temple, 225 feet long, by 118 wide. (This is the building in the photograph, against which the fallen column rests.)

F. The circular Temple, of which we shall give a view in a subsequent Part. It is 32 feet in diameter.

G. A Doric column.

H H. The City Walls, about 4 miles in circuit.

I. The City Gates.

'One [stone] in the western wall, 69 feet in length, 13 in depth, and 18 feet in breadth, containing 16,146 cubic feet of stone. This measurement gives the enormous weight of 1240 tons for this one stone; and supposing it to be broken up suitable for road-making, there would be sufficient to load four such vessels as are employed in bringing coals from the north to London, or to fill a string of one-horse carts that would extend nearly five miles in length!'

FROM FRITH'S NOTES TO 610E

FACSIMILE REPRODUCTION OF FRITH'S NOTES TO PHOTOGRAPH 610E (OPPOSITE)

BAALBEC, *The Circular Temple c1857* 611

BAALBEC, *The Ruins* (FROM AN ENGRAVING)

Baalbek (Frith's Baalbec) lies to the north of Damascus in what is now Lebanon. Some idea of the difficulty of getting there in Frith's day is provided by the opening sentence of his account of the circular temple: he tells of two days' ride from Damascus, each of eleven or twelve hours. The site lies in the Beqa'a valley, and the name Baalbek probably means 'Baal, or Lord, of the Beqa'a'. The site dates back to the early Bronze Age, but all the ruins we see in the photographs are Roman. The temple was built at a time when the valley was extremely wealthy – it was one of the 'granaries' of Rome. It was one of the largest temple complexes of the ancient world, with sanctuaries dedicated to Jupiter and Bacchus; the circular temple was almost certainly dedicated to Venus, although no inscription proves this. It is first mentioned in Western sources by Henry Maundrell in his 'Journey from Aleppo to Jerusalem' in 1697. It was drawn by Robert Wood in 1757, and this is mentioned in Frith's commentary. The six free-standing columns are part of the immense Temple of Jupiter, of which little remains but its vast foundations. At the far left of photograph (610E, page 216), we can just see one of the wonders of the site, the three enormous stones making up the trilithon. Each block had a volume of 14000 cubic feet and a weight of about 1000 tons. To the right is a more complete temple, the Temple of Bacchus, which has a very well-preserved interior.

ABOVE: MOUNT HERMON, *From Hazor c2000*
BY KIND PERMISSION OF TODD BOLEN/BIBLEPLACES.COM

TOP: MOUNT LEBANON, *The Largest of the Cedars c1857* 615E

ABOVE: GEEZEH (GIZA) PLATEAU, *The Solar Boat of Khufu 2004* G318003K

On the flag of the Lebanon is the cedar tree. From the earliest times these imposing trees have provided wood for building in the eastern Mediterranean. Frith wrote in his notes to this scene that he had passed a wonderful day in their shade, and he went on to mention the Biblical references to these trees. But it was not only David's temple that had beams of cedar; the doors of Egyptian temples were often made of cedar wood, and the boat of Khufu at Giza is also made of the trunks of huge straight cedar trees.

BANIAS, *The Ancient Caesarea Philippi c1857* 603E

BANIAS, *Caesarea Philippi, Waterfall* 2000
BY KIND PERMISSION OF TODD BOLEN/BIBLEPLACES.COM

Situated 25 miles north of the Sea of Galilee and at the base of Mount Hermon, Caesarea Philippi (603E, opposite) is the location of one of the largest springs feeding the Jordan River. Here water plunges from the rocks of the Golan Heights. As with many springs, this place had religious associations from the earliest times. In Old Testament times it had links with the Canaanite god Baal, while its name derives from a link with the Greek god Pan. This is the place where, according to Matthew, Jesus was transfigured and where he revealed his eventual fate. It was a provincial capital under the Herodian Kings, and thus gained great size, eventually covering an area of seven hundred acres. It is not clear today what or where the ruins in Frith's picture are.

'A panther carried off a goat from a flock within a walled enclosure about fifty yards from our tent. He leapt the wall, with his victim over his shoulder; the ball fired by the man who was watching the flock passing so close, that we distinctly heard its "whizz" over the roof of our tent.'

FRITH'S NOTES TO PHOTOGRAPH 603E *(opposite)*

Banias is situated about midway on the road usually taken by travellers between Tiberias and Damascus. The village, as described by Dr. Robinson, occupies a terrace 1147 feet above the sea. He says – 'The situation of Banias is unique, combining in an unusual degree the elements of grandeur and beauty. It nestles in its recess at the southern base of the mighty Hermon, which towers in majesty to an elevation of seven or eight thousand feet above. Its terrace I have already described, over which the abundant waters of the glorious fountain spread luxuriant fertility, and the graceful interchange of copse, lawn, and waving fields. The situation is charming. Lying so high above the Huleh, its atmosphere partakes of the salubrity of the adjacent mountain. The vicinity of the mountain, the many woods, and the rich fields of grain around Banias, make it the resort of an abundance of game. Panthers and wolves are on the mountains; wild swine and gazelles luxuriate among the grain. Wild ducks, partridges, snipe, and other birds, are in plenty.'

With regard to the animals mentioned by Dr. Robinson, I will relate my own experience in this district. Whilst our men were pitching the tents in the plain below Banias, near the brink of the Lake Merom, I took my gun, and strolled up the side of the mountain, in the hope of meeting with partridges; but, instead of birds, I very soon put up, at the same instant, and apparently feeding close together, a wild boar and a gazelle. A good rifle-shot might have killed both. Descending, I saw a wolf prowling, with remarkable coolness, around our tents. We killed a large black snake close to the encampment; and I saw on the mountain two others of a brown colour, and each of them about ten feet long. Two nights afterwards, at Beit Jeun, on the other side of Banias, a panther carried off a goat from a flock within a walled enclosure about fifty yards from our tent. He leapt the wall, with his victim over his shoulder; the ball fired by the man who was watching the flock passing so close, that we distinctly heard its 'whizz' over the roof of our tent.

NABLOUS, *The Ancient Shechem c1857* 591E (DETAIL)

Frith's pictures of Nablous differ in angle from those of David Roberts; they more closely resemble those of W H Bartlett, whose images were published in 1847 in 'A Christian in Palestine' by Henry Stebbing. It is an interesting coincidence that the book was published by Frith's later publisher, George Virtue.

At the time these photographs were taken (591 and 591E), the ancient Shechem was thought to be Nablous. Shechem was the place where Abraham first entered Canaan, and here God appeared to him. Jacob lived in Shechem, and handed it on to his son Joseph. It is the site of Jacob's well, now covered by a Greek Orthodox Church. In fact, the ancient town has been shown by more recent archaeology to lie closer to the nearby town of Tel Balata.

NABLOUS, *Jacob's Well near Shechem c1861* 591

TIBERIAS, *The Town and the Lake from the North c1857* 600E

For Frith, Tiberias was intimately associated with the Gospels, as the town stands on the Sea of Galilee. It was founded in AD 20 by Herod Antipas, and was dedicated to the Roman Emperor Tiberius. As well as having links to the Gospels, the town has a major role in Jewish history. The town played no part in the Jewish revolt (it surrendered to the Romans), but after the destruction of the second temple in AD 70, Jewish courts moved here, thus making Tiberias a centre of Jewish learning. The ruins we see here were almost certainly caused by an earthquake in 749. This destroyed a church, which was then rebuilt. Today the town is a popular tourist resort – it is on the Sea of Galilee and close to hot springs.

TIBERIAS, *From the South c1857* 601E

FRITH'S NOTES TO PHOTOGRAPH 600E *(opposite)*

I judge that the waters of the lake have encroached considerably upon the Roman town of Tiberias, or else that the sea-wall has crumbled away, leaving the towers or bastions only standing far out into the water. From one of these remaining masses of old Roman masonry, nearly the most southernly one, the present view is taken. These ruins (which are portions of the walls of the old town), and the castle seen in the view, at the northern extremity, constitute the most striking features of the place at the present day. The town itself is a most wretchedly forlorn and dirty-looking assemblage of houses, or hovels of ultra-oriental character. The population is about 3000, of whom perhaps one-fourth are Jews. There is an adage, 'that the king of the fleas holds his court in Tiberias.' This we had vividly in mind on our arrival at the spot, and so were steeled against the strong inclination of our Bedouins to pitch our tents within the walls.

Escaping this infliction, we arranged that the clear blue waters of the hallowed lake should almost wash the threshold of our tents, which were pitched a little to the south of the place from which my view is taken. We enjoyed a most refreshing bathe; and whilst taking my view I could see multitudes of fine fish in the bright water below. There are five different kinds of fish in this lake, all of good quality. It will be remembered that here was the scene of the miraculous draught of fishes: yet there is now only one crazy old boat on the lake! I detected, by the difficulty which I found in using the water of the lake for photographic purposes, that it is impregnated with a considerable quantity of saline matter. The same, of course, may be said of the water of the Jordan, which runs from this lake to the Dead Sea; yet the salt is not in sufficient quantity to render the water unpleasant to the taste.

There probably existed no town upon this identical spot in the days of Our Saviour. It was built, as its name indicates, during the reign of the Emperor Tiberias, by the Tetrarch, Herod Antipas, and long remained the capital of the province, being, along with Sephoris, one of the two largest cities of Galilee. After the destruction of Jerusalem, Tiberias was celebrated, during several centuries, for its famous rabbinical academy. The modern name is Tabaria. It suffered greatly by an earthquake on New Year's Day, 1837, when almost every building, with the exception of the walls and the castle, was levelled to the ground; and up to the present time - such are the poverty and indolence of the inhabitants - scarcely any repairs have taken place. Dr. Robinson says that the Jews who inhabit this place are chiefly from Russian Poland - Tiberias and the neighbouring city of Safed being the two holy cities of the modern Jews in Galilee; Jerusalem and Hebron in Judea. The Lake of Tiberias, or, as it is often called in Scripture, the Sea of Galilee, is about eleven miles long, with an average width of about four miles. Its surface is depressed below that of the Mediterranean about 750 feet - the depression of the Dead Sea being 1316 feet. Thus the river Jordan, in its course of 56 geographical miles between the two lakes, falls 566 feet ...

DAMASCUS, *A Distant View c1857* 604E

TIBERIAS, *From the North c2000*

BY KIND PERMISSION OF TODD BOLEN/BIBLEPLACES.COM

DAMASCUS, *The Street called Straight c1857* 533E

'To the eye it is undoubtedly a magnificent view: the white buildings of the city, covering a vast area, glitter charmingly through the interminable plain of rich foliage.'

FRITH'S NOTES TO PHOTOGRAPH 604E *(opposite)*

It has been stated in a previous article upon Damascus that its details are likely to disappoint the traveller, and in presenting this attempt at the celebrated view of the city and plain from the slope of Lebanon, we must qualify the disappointment of our friends who have read the glowing descriptions of this scene given by a score of travellers, by acknowledging that the camera does very scanty justice – we might almost say does an injustice – to subjects so distant, and so minute and indistinct in their details as this is; but had we not attempted it (though on a very rough, unfavourable day), we should, in all probability, have suffered the heavy displeasure of the critics who have read of such a scene, or possibly even beheld it. To the eye it is undoubtedly a magnificent view: the white buildings of the city, covering a vast area, glitter charmingly through the interminable plain of rich foliage - the elevation, shortly after the traveller leaves the village of Salihiyeh for Beyrout or Baalbec, being sufficient to give him a splendid range of vision. The plain upon which Damascus stands, and which is watered chiefly by the snow-fed streams of the Barada (Abana) and A'waj (Pharpar), is of uknown extent, having been in modern times but very imperfectly explored. Mr. Porter has published some very interesting information respecting its eastern tracts, where it holds the basins of three mighty lakes, which have no outlets, but are the natural receptacles for the waters of all the rivers and fountains of the plain of Damascus; each lake is about two miles in circumference.

From the furthest point reached in this direction, Mr. Porter described numerous mounds and other objects, which had the appearance of being the sites of ruined cities; and during the summer of last year Cyril Graham, an enterprising young traveller, who was accompanied only by his servant, reports, in the district of the Hauran, to the north and east of the lakes above named, the discovery of the sites of about eighty cities of very great apparent antiquity.

Damascus, although certainly one of the oldest inhabited sites in the world (in the days of Abraham it was already a city of note) has suffered many spoliations, and a few almost entire demolitions, from the "chances of war"; very little, as we have before had occasion to remark, now remaining of great antiquity within its walls. It has also suffered to some extent from earthquakes.

Damascus has had a long association with the beginnings of Christianity. 'The Street called Straight' was the location of the house Saul was staying in when he was converted by Ananias. It had immense resonance for Frith, therefore. Not only does this street have Biblical links, but it was also the Roman Via Recta, which stretched for one mile lined with columns with gates at both ends. It still exists in modern Damascus, but it is now divided into two in the old part of the city, Avenue of Bab Sharqi and the Souk Medhat Pasha.

Although Frith took pains to link Damascus with the Bible in his commentaries, he seems also to have been somewhat disappointed with the place. He acknowledges in the notes to photograph 604E that the photograph does not do justice to the view, while in the later part of the same notes we get the distinct impression that the city had in the eyes of Frith seen better days: it had suffered 'many spoliations and a few almost entire demolitions.' Reputedly one of the oldest inhabited cities in the world, Damascus has had the familiar chequered history that other cities in the Middle East have had. In the era before Christ it changed hands many times: it was ruled in turn by the Aramean kings, the Assyrians, and the Arkhenaeans, amongst others. It was ruled by the Nabateans until the Romans took over in AD 105. With the decline of the Roman Empire, it came under Byzantine rule until AD 635, when the Arab Moslems gained power. Since then, many different groups have ruled; the most successful were the Omayyads, who instigated a great building programme. After their fall in AD 749, the city went into something of a decline. It was really at the end of this time that Frith visited.

Further Reading

Most of the following books are generally available, and most are general introductions. They do not represent an exhaustive bibliography for the text nor the subject.

Ancient Egypt

Peter Clayton. *Chronicle of the Pharaohs.* Thames and Hudson 1994
Richard H Wilkinson. *The Complete Temples of Ancient Egypt.* Thames and Hudson 2000
Dieter Arnold. *The Encyclopaedia of Ancient Egyptian Architecture.* Tauris 2003
Stephen Quirke, ed. *The Temple in Ancient Egypt.* British Museum 1997
Ian Shaw and Paul Nicholson. *The British Museum Dictionary of Ancient Egypt.* British Museum 1995
William MacQuitty. *Island of Isis. Philae Temple of the Nile.* Macdonald and James 1976
Eugen Strouhal. *Life of the Ancient Egyptians.* Liverpool University Press 1997
RB Parkinson. *Voices from Ancient Egypt.* British Museum 1991
J R Harris, ed. *The Legacy of Egypt.* Oxford University Press 1988
Paul Lipke. *The Royal Ship of Cheops.* BAR International Series 1984
N Jenkins. *The Boat Beneath the Pyramid.* Thames and Hudson 1980

Ancient Egypt, the Holy Land and Art

Berko and Meulienaere. *Ancient Egypt in Nineteenth Century Painting.* Berko 1992
Bourbon and Attini. *Yesterday and Today – Egypt. Lithographs and Diaries by David Roberts.* Swan Hill 1996
Jean-Marcel Humbert and Clifford Price, ed. *Imhotep Today: Egyptianizing Architecture.* UCL Press 2003
James Stevens Curl. *Egyptomania. The Egyptian Revival: a Recurring Theme in the History of Taste.* Manchester University Press 1994
Douglas R Nickel. *Francis Frith in Egypt and Palestine – A Victorian Photographer Abroad.* Princeton University Press 2004
Allen Staley and Christopher Newall. *Pre-Raphelite Vision: Truth to Nature.* Tate 2004

Orientalism, Travel and the Reception of Ancient Egypt

Roger Matthews and Cornelia Roeme, eds. *Ancient Perspectives on Egypt* eds. UCL Press 2003
Nicholas Warner, ed. *An Egyptian Panorama: Reports from the 19th Century British Press.* Zeitouna 1994
Paul and Janet Starkey, eds. *Interpreting the Orient: Travellers in Egypt and the Near East.* Ithaca 2001
Edward Said. *Orientalism: Western Concepts of the Orient.* Routledge Kegan & Paul 1978
Deborah Manley. *The Nile, a Traveller's Anthology.* Cassell 1991
Paul and Janet Starkey, eds. *Travellers in Egypt.* Taurus 1998
David Jeffereys, ed. *Views of Ancient Egypt since Napoleon Bonapart: imperialism, colonialism and modern appropriations.* UCL Press 2003

Israel, Palestine, Jerusalem and the Holy Land

B S J Isserlin. *The Israelites.* Thames and Hudson 1998
Michael D Coogan, ed. *The Oxford History of the Biblical World.* Oxford University Press 1998
Ian Wilson. *The Bible is History.* Weidenfeld and Nicholson 1999
Dan Bahat & Chim Rabinstein. *Illustrated Atlas of Jerusalem.* Simon and Shuster 1990
Kathleen Kenyon. *Jerusalem: excavating 3000 years of History.* Thames and Hudson 1967
Friederich Ragette. *Baalbek.* Chatto and Windus 1980
John Day. *The Oxford Bible Atlas.* Oxford University Press 1984
Kathleen Stuart Howe. *Revealing the Holy Land.* Santa Barbara Museum of Art 1997.

Guide Books

John Rodenbeck, ed. *Cairo – Insight Guide.* APA publications 1996
Dorothy Stannard, ed. *Egypt – Insight Guide.* APA Publications 2000
Soraya Khalidy, ed. *Egypt – Everyman Guide.* David Campbell 1995
Jill Kamil. *Luxor: A Guide to Ancient Thebes.* Egyptian International Publishing – Longman 1996
Jill Kamil. *Sakkara and Memphis: The Necropolis and the Ancient Capital.* Egyptian International Publishing – Longman 1996

Francis Frith – A Brief Biography

Francis Frith 1822–1898

FRANCIS FRITH, founder of the world-famous photographic archive, was a complex and multi-talented man. A devout Quaker and a highly successful Victorian businessman, he was philosophic by nature and pioneering in outlook. By 1855 he had already established a wholesale grocery business in Liverpool, and sold it for the astonishing sum of £200,000, which is the equivalent today of over £15,000,000. Now in his thirties, and captivated by the new science of photography, Frith set out on a series of pioneering journeys up the Nile and to the Near East.

Intrigue and exploration

He was the first photographer to venture beyond the sixth cataract of the Nile. Africa was still the mysterious 'Dark Continent', and Stanley and Livingstone's historic meeting was a decade into the future. The conditions for picture taking confound belief. He laboured for hours in his wicker dark-room in the sweltering heat of the desert, while the volatile chemicals fizzed dangerously in their trays. Back in London he exhibited his photographs and was 'rapturously cheered' by members of the Royal Society. His reputation as a photographer was made overnight.

Venture of a Life-Time

By the 1870s the railways had threaded their way across the country, and Bank Holidays and half-day Saturdays had been made obligatory by Act of Parliament. All of a sudden the working man and his family were able to enjoy days out, take holidays, and see a little more of the world.

With typical business acumen, Francis Frith foresaw that these new tourists would enjoy having souvenirs to commemorate their days out. For the next thirty years he travelled the country by train and by pony and trap, producing fine photographs of seaside resorts and beauty spots that were keenly bought by millions of Victorians. These prints were painstakingly pasted into family albums and pored over during the dark nights of winter, rekindling precious memories of summer excursions.

Frith's studio was soon supplying retail shops all over the country. To meet the demand he gathered about him a small team of photographers, and published the work of independent artist-photographers of the calibre

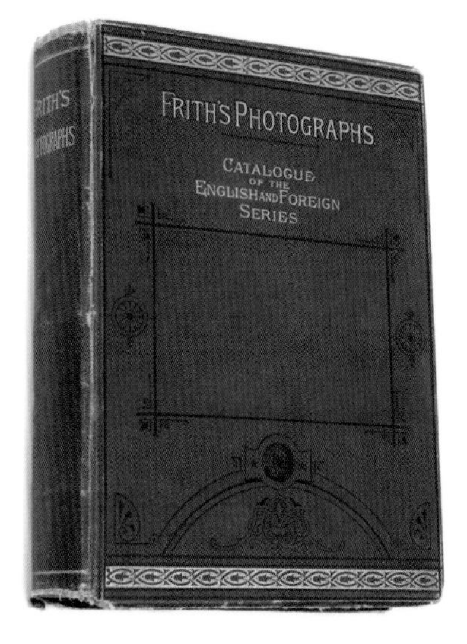

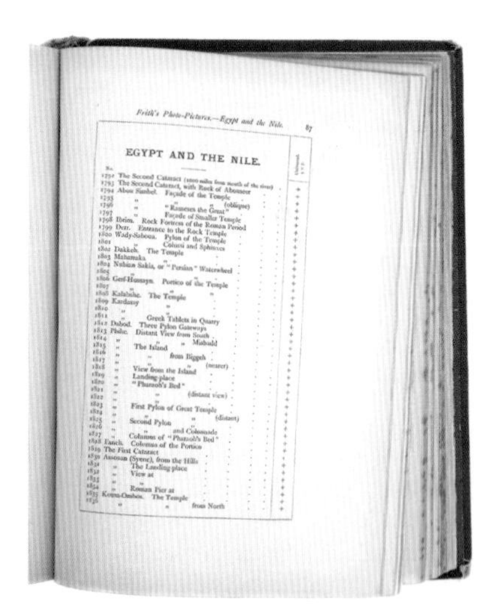

F Frith & Co 1886 catalogue, with sample page of Egyptian photographs.

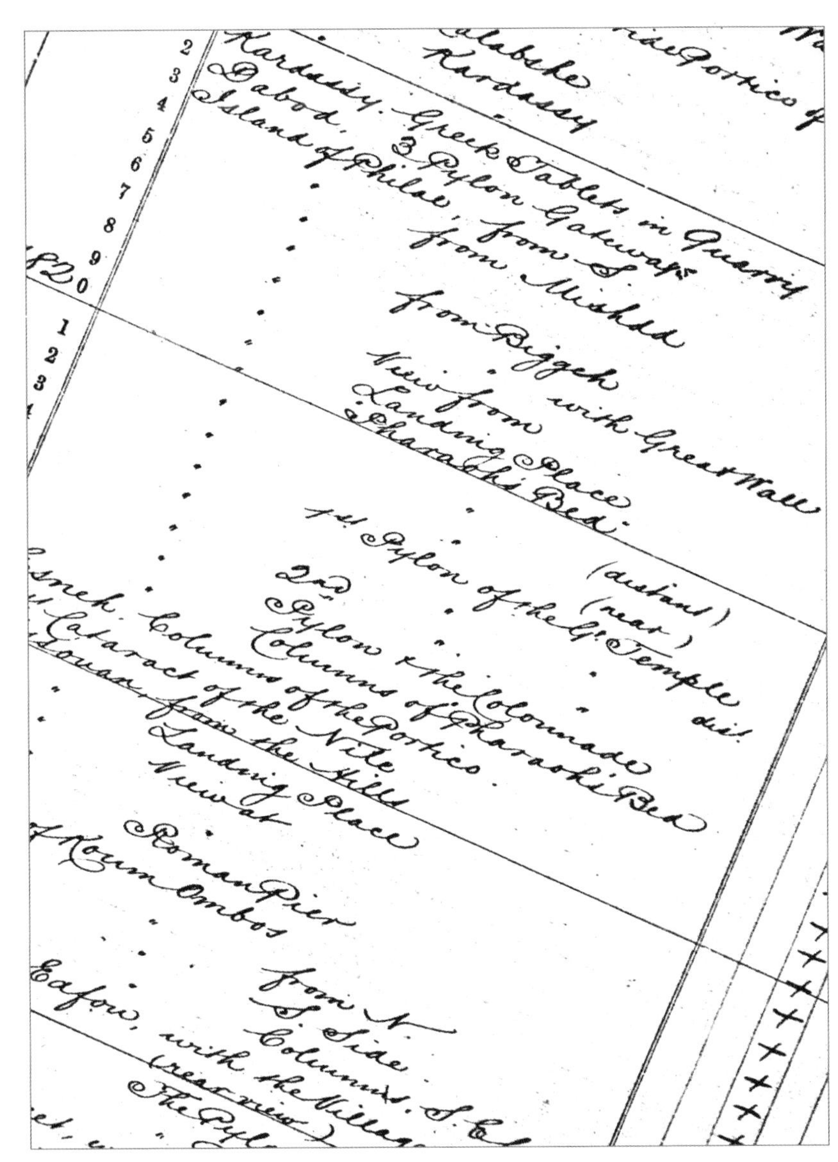
Kardassy. Greek Tablets in Quarry
Dabod. 3 Pylon Gateways
Island of Philae, from S.
from Mishdd
from Biggeh with Great Wall
View from Landing Place
Pharaoh's Bed
1st Pylon of the Gt. Temple (distant)
2nd (near)
Pylon & the Colonnade
Columns of the Portico.
Cataract of the Nile
Landing Place
Roman Pier
Kom Ombos
from N.
S. Side.
Columns. S.E.

A page from the F Frith & Co hand-written ledgers, detailing photographs taken of Egypt.

of Roger Fenton and Francis Bedford. In order to gain some understanding of the scale of Frith's business one only has to look at the catalogue issued by Frith & Co in 1886: it runs to some 670 pages, listing not only many thousands of views of the British Isles but also many photographs of most European countries, and Egypt, China, Japan, the USA and Canada. Note, too, the sample page shown here from the hand-written *Frith & Co* ledgers detailing pictures of Egypt taken. By 1890 Frith had created the greatest specialist photographic publishing company in the world, with over 2,000 outlets – more than the combined number that Boots and WH Smith have today!

Francis Frith's Legacy

Francis Frith had died in 1898 at his villa in Cannes, his great project still growing. The archive he created continued in business for another seventy years. By 1970 it contained over a third of a million pictures showing 7,000 British towns and villages.

Frith's legacy to us today is of immense significance and value, for the magnificent archive of evocative photographs he created provides a unique record of change in the cities, towns and villages throughout Britain over a century and more. Frith and his fellow studio photographers revisited locations many times down the years to update their views, compiling for us an enthralling and colourful pageant of British life and character.

We are fortunate that Frith was dedicated to recording the minutiae of everyday life. For it is this sheer wealth of visual data, the painstaking chronicle of changes in dress, transport, street layouts, buildings, housing, engineering and landscape that captivates us so much today, offering us a powerful link with the past and with the lives of our ancestors.

The F Frith & Co retailer display board, showing six of the company's photographic prints.

Computers have now made it possible for Frith's many thousands of images to be accessed almost instantly. The archive offers every one of us an opportunity to examine the places where we and our families have lived and worked down the years. Its images, depicting our shared past, are now bringing pleasure and enlightenment to millions around the world a century and more after his death.

Francis Frith with his wife and children.

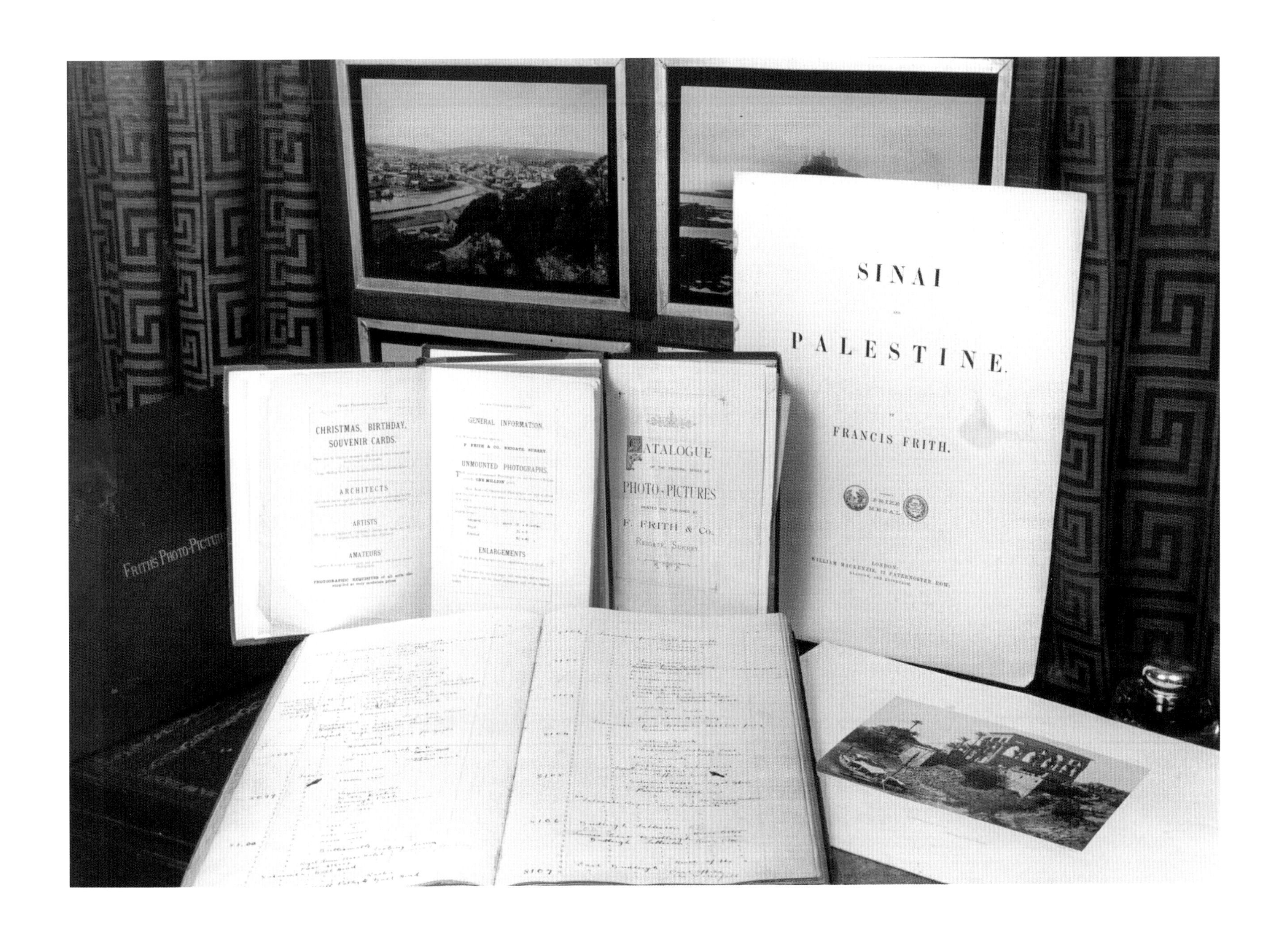
CHRISTMAS, BIRTHDAY, SOUVENIR CARDS.
ARCHITECTS
ARTISTS
AMATEURS
GENERAL INFORMATION
UNMOUNTED PHOTOGRAPHS
ENLARGEMENTS
CATALOGUE
PHOTO-PICTURES
F. FRITH & Co.
REIGATE, SURREY
SINAI
PALESTINE.
FRANCIS FRITH.
LONDON.

The Author

Richard Lunn has been fascinated by ancient Egypt for a number of years. He taught himself to read hieroglyphs, working on a translation of the 'Dream Stele', an inscribed tablet between the paws of the Sphinx, before studying for a master's degree in Egyptian archaeology at University College, London.

He was a contributor to 'Imhotep Today', a book discussing the influence of ancient Egyptian architecture on today's built environment, published by UCL Press.

He has travelled to Egypt regularly, and lectures to Egyptian and archaeological societies. His main interests in the field are the everyday life and art of ancient Egypt, and the relationships between the countries of the West and ancient and modern Egypt.